BASEBALL TRIVIA

Publications International, Ltd.

Written by Lisa Brooks

Photography from Shutterstock.com

Louis Weber, CEO
Publications International, Ltd.
8140 Lehigh Avenue
Morton Grove, IL 60053

ISBN: 978-1-68022-869-4

Manufactured in China.

8 7 6 5 4 3 2 1

TABLE OF CONTENTS

BASEBALL BASICS

1. How many innings are played in a game of professional baseball?
   A. Six
   B. Seven
   C. Eight
   D. Nine

2. The line around the bases is called the diamond. How many total feet does the diamond encompass?
   A. 320
   B. 360
   C. 380
   D. 400

3. What is another term for the defensive team in baseball?
   A. Fielding team
   B. Home team
   C. Running team
   D. Throwing team

ANSWERS

1.   **D. Nine**

College baseball games are also nine innings; but high schoolers play seven innings, and players in Little League baseball play six-inning games.

2.   **B. 360**

A baseball diamond is 90 feet square, making the total perimeter 360 feet.

3.   **A. Fielding team**

The fielding team attempts to prevent baserunners from scoring.

QUESTIONS

4. The area where a pitcher aims to throw the ball is called what?

        A. Batting area

        B. Hit zone

        C. Ball target

        D. Strike zone

5. What is the name of the field outside the first and third baselines?

        A. Sidelines

        B. Foul territory

        C. Outfield

        D. Back field

6. What is the name of the player whose position is behind home plate?

        A. Shortstop

        B. Pitcher

        C. Catcher

        D. Pitching coach

ANSWERS

4.   D. Strike zone

The strike zone is determined by a batter's stance, but is generally an area with a limit between the batter's knees and chest.

5.   B. Foul territory

While the area beyond the baselines is foul, the lines themselves are considered fair territory.

6.   C. Catcher

The catcher, as the name suggests, catches a pitched ball when the batter fails to hit it.

QUESTIONS

7. What is the name of a pitch which does not enter the strike zone and is not swung at by the batter?

     A. Balk

     B. Strike

     C. Ball

     D. Out

8. The first, second, and third bases are 15-inch square bags. What shape is home plate?

     A. Square

     B. Pentagon

     C. Circle

     D. Octagon

9. What is the name for the area where the batter stands while waiting for a pitch?

     A. Pitch square

     B. Batting cage

     C. Bat area

     D. Batter's box

ANSWERS

7.   C. Ball

The batter is awarded with an advancement to first base if the pitcher throws four balls before the batter is out.

8.   B. Pentagon

The five-sided home plate is usually made of rubber, and is about 17 inches wide.

9.   D. Batter's box

There are two batter's boxes, one on each side of home plate, which are 4 feet wide and 6 feet long.

QUESTIONS

10. Which letter is used to indicate a strikeout?
> A. S
> B. O
> C. K
> D. T

11. How far is the distance between the middle of the pitcher's mound and home plate?
> A. 60 feet
> B. 60 feet, 6 inches
> C. 62 feet
> D. 62 feet, 3 inches

12. Which of the following is NOT the name of a pitch used in baseball?
> A. Cutter
> B. Screwball
> C. Forkball
> D. Slicer

ANSWERS

10.   C. K

English-born sportswriter Henry Chadwick is credited with the "K" letter designation for strikeouts. He chose "K" because it is the last letter in "struck," and "S" was already used to indicate "sacrifice."

11.   B. 60 feet, 6 inches

The specific distance was set by rule makers in 1893.

12.   D. Slicer

Other pitches include the fastball, curveball, sinker, and slider.

QUESTIONS

13. What is the term for a batter who replaces another batter?

    A. Pinch hitter
    B. Switch hitter
    C. Replacement
    D. New batter

14. How many innings must be played before a game can be considered an official game?

    A. Four
    B. Five
    C. Seven
    D. Nine

15. How many teams make up Major League Baseball?

    A. 26
    B. 28
    C. 30
    D. 32

ANSWERS

13.   A. Pinch hitter

A team may substitute for a player as long as the ball is not in play. Pinch runners may also be used to replace baserunners.

14.   B. Five

If five innings have been completed and the game is called due to weather or some other reason, the game still counts as an official regulation game. But if fewer than five innings have been played, the game is postponed and replayed at another time.

15.   C. 30

As of 2017, there are a total of 30 teams in MLB: 15 in the American League and 15 in the National League.

QUESTIONS

16. True or false:

The home team always goes to bat first.

17. True or false:

First base and home plate are the only bases that runners may overrun.

18. True or false:

The shortstop plays in the field between first and second base.

19. True or false:

The pitcher must keep one foot on the "pitcher's rubber" throughout the entire pitch.

20. True or false:

The right fielder's position is behind third base, and the left fielder's is behind first base.

ANSWERS

16. False

The visiting team bats first, in the top of the inning, and the home team bats second, in the bottom of the inning.

17. True

Runners are allowed to overrun first base, to give them a better chance to beat a thrown ball. And they may overrun home plate, since that's the final base. But second and third bases may not be overrun – so if a runner runs past either of those bases, they must continue to the next base.

18. False

The shortstop is positioned between second and third base.

19. True

Because the pitcher must keep one foot on the 24-inch by 6-inch plate on top of the pitcher's mound, he can only take one step before throwing.

20. False

The positions of the fielders are according to what the catcher sees when looking out at the field. So the right fielder is behind first base, and the left fielder is behind third.

WORLD SERIES

1. What year was the first World Series played?
  A. 1903
  B. 1910
  C. 1914
  D. 1924

2. Which team has won the most World Series titles?
  A. Boston Red Sox
  B. Los Angeles Dodgers
  C. New York Yankees
  D. San Francisco Giants

3. In what year was the series first broadcast on television?
  A. 1946
  B. 1947
  C. 1948
  D. 1949

ANSWERS

1. **A. 1903**

The best-of-nine series was played between the Pittsburgh Pirates and the Boston Americans. Boston won, five games to three.

2. **C. New York Yankees**

As of 2016, the Yankees have played in 40 World Series and won 27 titles.

3. **B. 1947**

The series was broadcast on the brand-new NBC Television Network, which aired in New York, Philadelphia, Baltimore, and Washington, D.C., and was sponsored by Ford and Gillette.

QUESTIONS

4. Which player holds the record for the most walks in a single World Series?

     A. Willie Randolph

     B. Barry Bonds

     C. Joe Gordon

     D. Hank Thompson

5. Which baseball great hit the first pinch-hit home run in World Series history?

     A. Yogi Berra

     B. Joe Jackson

     C. Ted Williams

     D. Ty Cobb

6. What kind of animal supposedly "cursed" the Chicago Cubs during the 1945 World Series?

     A. Cat

     B. Horse

     C. Goat

     D. Sheep

ANSWERS

4.   B. Barry Bonds

Bonds walked in 13 of his 30 plate appearances during the 2002 World Series.

5.   A. Yogi Berra

The Yankees power hitter stepped in for catcher Sherm Lollar in the seventh inning of game three in the 1947 series.

6.   C. Goat

As the story goes, Billy Goat Tavern owner Billy Sianis brought his pet goat, Murphy, to Wrigley Field for game four of the 1945 World Series between the Chicago Cubs and the Detroit Tigers. Murphy, being a goat, smelled much less pleasant than the humans surrounding him. Fans, bothered by the olfactory assault, began to complain. Sianis and his goat were asked to leave, and an angry Sianis (on behalf of his offended goat) declared that the Cubs "ain't gonna win no more." The Cubs lost the 1945 series, and it took the team another 71 years to break "The Curse of the Billy Goat"!

QUESTIONS

7. Two managers each won seven World Series games during the course of their managerial careers. One was Joe McCarthy, and who was the other?

    A. Tommy Lasorda
    B. Casey Stengel
    C. Buck Showalter
    D. Miller Huggins

8. As of 2016, which is the only American League team that has never appeared in a World Series?

    A. Texas Rangers
    B. Tampa Bay Rays
    C. Minnesota Twins
    D. Seattle Mariners

9. The Boston Red Sox won the World Series in 2004. Before that, when was the last year they'd won?

    A. 1909
    B. 1918
    C. 1922
    D. 1927

ANSWERS

7. B. Casey Stengel

McCarthy managed the Yankees from 1931 to 1946, and Stengel was the team manager from 1949 to 1960.

8. D. Seattle Mariners

Even though they have yet to play in a World Series, in 2001 the Mariners tied the record for most games won in a single season—an impressive 116—with the Chicago Cubs.

9. B. 1918

According to baseball superstition, the Red Sox were cursed after they traded Babe Ruth to the New York Yankees.

QUESTIONS

10. Who is the youngest World Series MVP?
    A. Lew Burdette
    B. Sandy Koufax
    C. Bret Saberhagen
    D. Johnny Bench

11. Which pitcher holds the record for consecutive scoreless innings pitched in a World Series?
    A. Bob Gibson
    B. Whitey Ford
    C. Mike Stanton
    D. Christy Mathewson

12. As of 2016, which is the only team to come back from a three-game loss in the playoffs to clinch the league 4-3?
    A. Boston Red Sox
    B. Chicago White Sox
    C. Oakland Athletics
    D. New York Yankees

ANSWERS

10.   C. Bret Saberhagen

Saberhagen, who pitched in the 1985 World Series for the Kansas City Royals, was 21 years, six months, 16 days old when he won the award. He pitched two complete games, including a shutout, and helped the Royals win the championship.

11.   B. Whitey Ford

Ford pitched 33 consecutive scoreless innings in 1961, breaking a record that had previously been held by Babe Ruth.

12.   Boston Red Sox

In 2004, it looked like the Red Sox would be going home without a title after losing three games in a row to the New York Yankees in the playoffs. But after a remarkable four-win comeback, the Red Sox went on to win their first World Series in 86 years.

QUESTIONS

13. As of the end of the 2016 season, how many teams have yet to win a World Series championship?

     A. Five

     B. Six

     C. Seven

     D. Eight

14. Which pitcher has played in more World Series games than any other?

     A. Mike Stanton

     B. Mariano Rivera

     C. Whitey Ford

     D. Jeff Nelson

15. Who is the oldest World Series MVP?

     A. Don Larsen

     B. Mickey Lolich

     C. Willie Stargell

     D. Steve Yeager

ANSWERS

13.   D. Eight

Eight teams are due for a win: the Tampa Bay Rays, Colorado Rockies, Seattle Mariners, Washington Nationals, San Diego Padres, Houston Astros, Milwaukee Brewers, and the Texas Rangers.

14.   B. Mariano Rivera

Rivera played in 24 World Series games before retiring in 2013.

15.   C. Willie Stargell

Stargell, of the Pittsburgh Pirates, was 39 years old when he earned the award at the 1979 World Series.

QUESTIONS

16. Who is the only athlete that has appeared in both a World Series and the Super Bowl?
    A. Bo Jackson
    B. Deion Sanders
    C. Walt Masters
    D. Brian Jordan

17. As of the end of the 2016 season, how many career World Series records does Mickey Mantle still hold?
    A. One
    B. Three
    C. Five
    D. Seven

18. As of 2016, which is the only National League team that has never appeared in a World Series?
    A. Miami Marlins
    B. Washington Nationals
    C. Colorado Rockies
    D. Arizona Diamondbacks

ANSWERS

16.   B. Deion Sanders

Sanders played with the Atlanta Braves in the 1992 World Series, and he also played with both the San Francisco 49ers in the 1995 Super Bowl and the Dallas Cowboys in the 1996 Super Bowl.

17.   D. Seven

Mantle holds records for most runs scored (42), total bases (123), home runs (18), extra-base hits (26), RBIs (40), walks (43), and strikeouts (54). But it should be noted that he appeared in 12 World Series!

18.   B. Washington Nationals

The Nationals began in 1969 as the Montreal Expos. In 1994, they had the best record in baseball and were poised for a possible World Series appearance, but an MLB strike that began on August 12 resulted in the cancellation of the rest of the season, including the World Series.

QUESTIONS

19. True or false:
> The teams who play in the World Series have always been decided by post-season championship games.

20. True or false:
> Although common now, prior to the '70s very few World Series games were played at night.

21. True or false:
> The older National League has won more World Series championships than the American League.

22. True or false:
> In 1904, the year after the World Series debuted, the entire series was cancelled.

ANSWERS

19.   False

Prior to 1969, the World Series teams were chosen based on which team in each league had the best win-loss record. But since then, the American and National leagues each hold championship series to determine which teams will advance.

20.   True

The first night game of the World Series didn't occur until 1971. More fans had televisions by this point, and MLB realized they could get more viewers if the games were on after people came home from work and school.

21.   False

As of 2016, the American League leads the win total with 64 championships. The National League has won 48.

22.   True

The games should have been played between the New York Giants and the Boston Americans, but the Giants refused to play their bitter rivals. The New York/Boston rivalry continues to this day!

RECORD BREAKERS

1. Which player achieved a record-high batting average of .367?

      A. Babe Ruth
      B. Ty Cobb
      C. Barry Bonds
      D. Ted Williams

2. Who set a record for most runs batted in with 2,297?

      A. Hank Aaron
      B. Babe Ruth
      C. Stan Musial
      D. Barry Bonds

3. Which player set a record for most singles with 3,215?

      A. Ted Williams
      B. Tris Speaker
      C. Alex Rodriguez
      D. Pete Rose

ANSWERS

1.   B. Ty Cobb

Ty Cobb played with the Detroit Tigers from 1905 to 1926, and the Philadelphia Athletics from 1927 to 1928.

2.   A. Hank Aaron

After retiring from the field, Aaron took on front office roles with the Atlanta Braves. He was inducted into the National Baseball Hall of Fame in 1982.

3.   D. Pete Rose

Pete Rose played in the major leagues from 1963 to 1986. He then managed the Cincinnati Reds until 1989.

QUESTIONS

4. Which pitcher has a record of 511 wins?

     A. Roger Clemens

     B. Walter Johnson

     C. Cy Young

     D. Greg Maddux

5. Tris Speaker, a center fielder who played from 1907 to 1928, broke a record by hitting how many doubles?

     A. 654

     B. 689

     C. 756

     D. 792

6. Which player broke Hank Aaron's home run record?

     A. Alex Rodriguez

     B. Barry Bonds

     C. Albert Pujols

     D. Ken Griffey Jr.

ANSWERS

4. C. Cy Young

Denton True "Cy" Young played 22 seasons of baseball, from 1890 to 1911. A year after his death in 1955, the Cy Young Award was created to recognize the best pitchers in the game.

5. D. 792

Speaker, who played from 1907 to 1928, was inducted into the Baseball Hall of Fame in 1937.

6. B. Barry Bonds

Aaron held the home run record of 755 for 33 years before Bonds broke it. Bonds' record now stands at 762.

QUESTIONS

7. Sam Crawford, an outfielder with the Cincinnati Reds and the Detroit Tigers in the early days of MLB, still holds the record for most what?

    A. Triples

    B. RBIs

    C. Walks

    D. Inside-the-park home runs

8. San Francisco Giants pitcher Madison Bumgarner broke what unusual record?

    A. Most balks

    B. Least walks

    C. Highest ERA

    D. Most grand slams hit by pitcher

9. Which pitcher has a record for the most losses, with 316?

    A. Cy Young

    B. Randy Johnson

    C. Lefty Grove

    D. Warren Spahn

ANSWERS

7.   A. Triples

Crawford earned 309 triples throughout his career. As of 2016, the contemporary player with the most triples is Carl Crawford, with 123. The two Crawfords are of no relation!

8.   D. Most grand slams hit by pitcher

Bumgarner, who has hit three grand slams, has also helped the Giants win three World Series championships, in 2010, 2012, and 2014.

9.   A. Cy Young

It may seem surprising that the same player who holds the record for most wins also has the record for most losses. But Young also holds the record for most innings pitched, at just over 7,354.

QUESTIONS

10. Pitcher Orel Hershiser broke the record for consecutive scoreless innings, with how many?

    A. 45

    B. 49

    C. 59

    D. 63

11. Which lightning-fast left fielder broke a record with his 2,295 runs scored?

    A. Ryan Braun

    B. Rickey Henderson

    C. Brett Gardner

    D. Manny Ramirez

12. Which famous Boston Red Sox player broke a record with the highest on-base percentage of .482?

    A. Ted Williams

    B. Babe Ruth

    C. David Ortiz

    D. Carl Yastrzemski

ANSWERS

10.   C. 59

While playing with the Los Angeles Dodgers in 1988, Hershiser pitched from August 30 to September 28 without allowing a run. He helped lead the Dodgers to a World Series championship later that year.

11.   B. Rickey Henderson

Henderson, who retired in 2003, is still considered one of baseball's best leadoff hitters and baserunners.

12.   A. Ted Williams

Williams finished his career, which was spent entirely with the Red Sox, with a batting average of .344 and 521 home runs.

QUESTIONS

13. A player's slugging percentage is calculated by dividing total bases by total at bats. Which power hitter's career slugging percentage was .690?

    A. Babe Ruth
    B. David Ortiz
    C. Willie Mays
    D. Barry Bonds

14. Babe Ruth held the record for a single-season slugging percentage of .849 until which player broke his record?

    A. Pete Rose
    B. Hank Aaron
    C. Barry Bonds
    D. Alex Rodriguez

15. Barry Bonds holds the record for most career intentional walks with how many?

    A. 602
    B. 634
    C. 667
    D. 688

ANSWERS

13.   **A. Babe Ruth**

*Ruth's nickname "The Sultan of Swat" was well-earned.
He was inducted into the Baseball Hall of Fame in 1936 as one of its
inaugural members.*

14.   **C. Barry Bonds**

*Bonds achieved a .863 slugging percentage in 2001, with 411 total
bases in 476 at bats.*

15.   **D. 688**

*This is understandable in the case of the record-breaking Bonds:
intentional walks are usually used to avoid a dangerous hitter in
favor of one less likely to produce a scoring play.*

QUESTIONS

16. A record 3,562 games were played by which multiple-record holder?

A. Pete Rose
B. Barry Bonds
C. Babe Ruth
D. Ty Cobb

17. Cal Ripken is famous for his record-breaking streak of 2,632 consecutive games played. Whose record did he break?

A. Rogers Hornsby
B. Tris Speaker
C. Jackie Robinson
D. Lou Gehrig

18. Washington Senators pitcher Walter Johnson, who played from 1907 to 1927, still holds what record?

A. Most strikeouts
B. Most shutouts
C. Most walks
D. Highest ERA

ANSWERS

16.   A. Pete Rose

Rose broke a record set by Boston Red Sox player Carl Yastrzemski, who played in 3,308 games.

17.   D. Lou Gehrig

Gehrig's record of 2,130 consecutive games stood for 56 years!

18.   B. Most shutouts

Johnson pitched 110 games in which the opposing team failed to score a run, including 23 shutouts against the Philadelphia Athletics alone.

QUESTIONS

19. Which catcher set a record for most pickoffs with 81?
  A. Johnny Bench
  B. Jorge Posada
  C. Ivan Rodriguez
  D. Mike Piazza

20. Which relief pitcher has a record-breaking 652 saves to his name?
  A. Trevor Hoffman
  B. Mariano Rivera
  C. Jonathan Papelbon
  D. Goose Gossage

21. Pitcher Jesse Orosco holds what record?
  A. Most innings pitched
  B. Most home runs allowed
  C. Most walks
  D. Most games pitched

ANSWERS

19.   C. Ivan Rodriguez

Rodriguez is often considered one of the best catchers to ever play baseball, and he was elected to the National Baseball Hall of Fame in January of 2017.

20.   B. Mariano Rivera

The New York Yankees closer relied on only one pitch – a cut fastball – to strike out opposing batters.

21.   D. Most games pitched

Orosco pitched in 1,252 games during a career that spanned from 1979 to 2003. He retired when he was 46, one of the oldest players in the game.

QUESTIONS

22. True or false:

The 1928 Boston Braves set a record by playing eight consecutive double-headers.

23. True or false:

Cy Young's record of 749 complete games pitched is often regarded as the baseball record least likely to be broken.

24. True or false:

Pitching saves did not become officially recognized statistics until 1969.

ANSWERS

22. False

The team actually played a record-breaking nine consecutive double headers that year! After being plagued with poor weather throughout much of the season, resulting in far more cancelled games than usual, the team found themselves needing to play 36 games in four weeks. The team ended up playing 15 double headers, nine of which were in a row!

23. True

In the early days of baseball, it was common, and even expected, for pitchers to pitch the complete game, barring injury. In modern baseball, however, it is rare for a starting pitcher to play an entire game, with relief pitchers and closers taking over in the later innings. Because of this, most modern-day pitchers pitch no more than a handful of complete games during an entire season, making Cy Young's record of 749 nearly untouchable.

24. True

Although the term "save" was being used as far back as 1952, no one paid much attention to the stat until baseball writer Jerome Holzman developed a formula for more accurately calculating saves. Even then, it took another nine years for MLB to keep an official record.

STADIUM STATS

1. Which current Major League Baseball stadium is the oldest, as of 2017?
    A. Yankee Stadium
    B. Wrigley Field
    C. Fenway Park
    D. Dodger Stadium

2. Which team calls Chase Field home?
    A. Arizona Diamondbacks
    B. Colorado Rockies
    C. Miami Marlins
    D. New York Mets

3. As of 2017, which stadium is the newest?
    A. AT&T Park
    B. PNC Park
    C. Marlins Park
    D. SunTrust Park

ANSWERS

1.   C. Fenway Park

Fenway Park in Boston, home of the Boston Red Sox, has been in use since 1912.

2.   A. Arizona Diamondbacks

Chase Field opened in 1998 for the Diamondbacks' debut season.

3.   D. SunTrust Park

SunTrust Park is home to the Atlanta Braves. Construction on the park was started in 2014, and the stadium was completed in time for 2017 Opening Day.

QUESTIONS

4. Which team's stadium has the largest seating capacity?
A. New York Yankees
B. Los Angeles Dodgers
C. Seattle Mariners
D. Atlanta Braves

5. What is the name of the stadium where the San Francisco Giants play?
A. Giants Stadium
B. Petco Park
C. AT&T Park
D. Progressive Field

6. Which team's stadium has the smallest seating capacity?
A. Pittsburgh Pirates
B. Colorado Rockies
C. San Francisco Giants
D. Tampa Bay Rays

ANSWERS

4.   B. Los Angeles Dodgers

Dodger Stadium in Los Angeles has a seating capacity of 56,000.

5.   C. AT&T Park

AT&T Park was originally named Pacific Bell Park, and then SBC Park. When SBC bought AT&T in 2006, the stadium was renamed once again.

6.   D. Tampa Bay Rays

Tropicana Field in St. Petersburg, Florida, seats only 31,042 fans.

QUESTIONS

7. As of 2017, how many stadiums do not have corporate names through naming rights deals?
   A. 8
   B. 9
   C. 10
   D. 11

8. How many Major League Baseball stadiums use artificial turf instead of grass?
   A. Two
   B. Three
   C. Four
   D. Five

9. What was the name of the stadium where the San Francisco Giants originally played?
   A. Bayside Park
   B. Giants Stadium
   C. Seals Stadium
   D. San Fran Field

ANSWERS

7.   **C. 10**

The stadiums include Angel Stadium of Anaheim, Dodger Stadium, Fenway Park, Kauffman Stadium, Marlins Park, Nationals Park, Oakland–Alameda County Coliseum, Oriole Park at Camden Yards, Wrigley Field, and Yankee Stadium.

8.   **A. Two**

Only Rogers Centre, home of the Toronto Blue Jays, and Tropicana Field, home of the Tampa Bay Rays, use artificial turf instead of grass.

9.   **C. Seals Stadium**

The Giants played in Seals Stadium from 1958 until 1959.

QUESTIONS

10. Which park has a wall in left field which has been dubbed the "Little Green Monster"?
A. Progressive Field
B. Safeco Field
C. Minute Maid Park
D. Dodger Stadium

11. Before the Miami Marlins began playing at Marlins Park, where did they play?
A. American Airlines Arena
B. Hard Rock Stadium
C. Joe Robbie Stadium
D. Lockhart Stadium

12. Who or what is Fenway Park named after?
A. The first owner of the Red Sox
B. A neighborhood in Boston
C. A shortstop from the 1920s
D. A department store

ANSWERS

10.   A. Progressive Field

At 19 feet high, the wall is dwarfed by Fenway Park's Green Monster, but it still proves to be the difference between a home run and a double for many batters!

11.   C. Joe Robbie Stadium

The stadium was a multi-purpose stadium that was also home to the Miami Dolphins football team.

12.   B. A neighborhood in Boston

Fenway Park is named after the Fenway-Kenmore neighborhood in Boston where the stadium is located.

QUESTIONS

13. Chicago's Guaranteed Rate Field is home to the Chicago White Sox. In which stadium did the White Sox originally play?

    A. Wrigley Field
    B. Comiskey Park
    C. Fuller Park
    D. McKinley Park

14. At which stadium do the Minnesota Twins play?

    A. Safeco Field
    B. PNC Park
    C. Target Field
    D. Comerica Park

15. Camden Yards is home to which team?

    A. Cincinnati Reds
    B. Baltimore Orioles
    C. New York Mets
    D. Detroit Tigers

ANSWERS

13.   B. Comiskey Park

The White Sox played at Comiskey Park from 1910 until 1990. The park was demolished in 1991, and a new Comiskey Park was built across the street. It was renamed U.S. Cellular Field in 2003 and Guaranteed Rate Field in 2016.

14.   C. Target Field

The Twins moved to Target Field in 2010, after 28 seasons at the Hubert H. Humphrey Metrodome.

15.   B. Baltimore Orioles

The full name of the stadium is Oriole Park at Camden Yards, and it is located in downtown Baltimore, Maryland.

QUESTIONS

16. Turner Field in Atlanta was named after media mogul Ted Turner. But Atlanta residents had wanted to name it after which baseball great?

A. Chipper Jones

B. Hank Aaron

C. Eddie Mathews

D. Terry Pendleton

17. Which team plays at Great American Ball Park?

A. Cincinnati Reds

B. Washington Nationals

C. Miami Marlins

D. Colorado Rockies

18. How high is the "Green Monster" at Fenway Park?

A. 30 feet, 3 inches

B. 33 feet, 5 inches

C. 35 feet, 1 inch

D. 37 feet, 2 inches

ANSWERS

16. B. Hank Aaron

Aaron played 21 seasons with the Braves. A section of the original Atlanta-Fulton County Stadium outfield wall, which Aaron's 715th home run flew over, still stands near Turner Field.

17. A. Cincinnati Reds

Perhaps the luckiest of all teams with corporate stadium names, the Reds' fitting stadium moniker comes from the Great American Insurance Group.

18. D. 37 feet, 2 inches

The high wall in left field is only 310 feet from home plate, and often results in batters hitting doubles that would be home runs in other stadiums.

QUESTIONS

19. Miller Park, home of the Milwaukee Brewers, is nicknamed what?

      A. The Brewhouse

      B. Beer Park

      C. The Keg

      D. Hoppywood

20. The New York Yankees play in a stadium in which New York borough?

      A. The Bronx

      B. Manhattan

      C. Brooklyn

      D. Staten Island

21. What was the original name of Rogers Centre in Toronto?

      A. CN Tower Arena

      B. Toronto Field

      C. Blue Jay Stadium

      D. SkyDome

ANSWERS

19.   C. The Keg

A fitting nickname for the park, which was named after the Miller Brewing Company!

20.   A. The Bronx

The team's location may have been obvious because of their famous nickname, "The Bronx Bombers."

21.   D. SkyDome

The name was chosen after a country-wide contest to name the stadium in 1987. The finalists were narrowed down to "Towerdome," Harbourdome," "The Dome," and the winning "SkyDome." The stadium was renamed Rogers Centre after it was purchased by Rogers Communications in 2005.

QUESTIONS

22. How many stadiums feature manually operated scoreboards?

    A. Zero

    B. One

    C. Two

    D. Three

23. What interesting feature is located behind the right field fence at Kauffman Stadium in Kansas City?

    A. A putting green

    B. A fountain

    C. A giant sculpture of a baseball glove

    D. An ice cream shop

24. Globe Life Park is home to which team?

    A. Pittsburgh Pirates

    B. Baltimore Orioles

    C. Texas Rangers

    D. Atlanta Braves

ANSWERS

22.   D. Three

Both Fenway Park and Wrigley Field are famous for their manual scoreboards. But lesser known is the manual board at the San Francisco Giant's AT&T Park: while the Giant's score is shown on a high-definition screen, the scores of other MLB games being played are displayed on a manually operated board in right field.

23.   B. A fountain

Kansas City is known for its abundance of fountains, and the fountain at Kauffman Stadium, known as the "Water Spectacular," is the largest privately funded fountain in the world.

24.   C. Texas Rangers

The stadium, located in Arlington, Texas, was known as The Ballpark in Arlington from 1994 until 2004, and then Ameriquest Field. A new stadium is now planned for the team, which is set to open in 2020.

QUESTIONS

25. Which team plays at Minute Maid Park?
   A. Tampa Bay Rays
   B. Houston Astros
   C. Arizona Diamondbacks
   D. Miami Marlins

26. The Colorado Rockies play at which stadium?
   A. Coors Field
   B. Busch Stadium
   C. AT&T Park
   D. SunTrust Park

ANSWERS

25.   B. Houston Astros

The stadium has undergone several name changes, including The Ballpark at Union Station, Enron Field, and Astros Field.

26.   A. Coors Field

The inaugural Rockies played their first two seasons at Mile High Stadium while Coors Field was being constructed. They've played in the park since 1995.

QUESTIONS

27. True or false:

The largest crowd to ever fill Busch Stadium in St. Louis was not in the stadium to watch a baseball game.

28. True or false:

Kauffman Stadium in Kansas City is the only MLB stadium named after a person.

29. True or false:

Rogers Centre in Toronto is the only MLB stadium without bleacher seating.

30. True or false:

Oakland-Alameda County Coliseum is the only remaining stadium that is home to both an MLB and NFL team.

ANSWERS

27. **True**

On May 23, 2003, more than 48,000 people filled the 43,975-capacity stadium to watch a soccer game between Manchester City Football Club and Chelsea Football Club.

28. **False**

Although Kauffman is the only American League stadium named after a person, the National League's Wrigley Field is named after chewing gum magnate William Wrigley Jr.

29. **True**

While Rogers Centre lacks the bleacher seating found at other parks, they have a unique option for watching games: a hotel is attached to the stadium, with 70 rooms overlooking the park. Much more comfortable than bleachers!

30. **True**

The stadium is home to the Oakland Athletics and also the Oakland Raiders.

HISTORY

1. What year was the earliest mention of baseball in American history?

        A. 1791

        B. 1801

        C. 1809

        D. 1818

2. The regulations that are often considered the precursors to today's baseball rules were called what?

        A. The Knickknack Rules

        B. The Ballplayer's Regulations

        C. The Knickerbocker Rules

        D. The Brooklyn Statutes

3. The baseball "pitch" was originally modeled after the motion used in what game?

        A. Croquet

        B. Ring toss

        C. Bowling

        D. Horseshoes

ANSWERS

1.   A. 1791

The game was mentioned in an ordinance in Pittsfield, Massachusetts, where playing the game was banned near the town's meeting house.

2.   C. The Knickerbocker Rules

The rules consisted of 20 regulations, and included the dimensions of the field, the definition of a foul ball, and a prohibition against throwing a ball at a runner to put him out.

3.   D. Horseshoes

Players "pitched" the ball in the same way one would toss a horseshoe.

QUESTIONS

4. Sports writer Henry Chadwick was a critic of a rule in the game called the "bound rule." What was the bound rule?

> A. It prohibited fielders from chasing after foul balls
> B. It stated that if a batted ball bounced once and a fielder caught it, the batter was out
> C. It allowed balls hit within an arbitrary boundary around the field to be called home runs
> D. It required a team to play only one pitcher per game

5. In what year was the first women's baseball team created?

> A. 1866
> B. 1870
> C. 1875
> D. 1890

6. Who is credited with organizing the first professional baseball team, the Cincinnati Red Stockings?

> A. Abner Doubleday
> B. Doc Adams
> C. William Hulbert
> D. Harry Wright

ANSWERS

4.   B. It stated that if a batted ball bounced once and a fielder caught it, the batter was out

In 1864, the bound rule was eliminated for fair balls, thanks in part to Chadwick's vocal disagreement. The rule persisted for foul balls until the 1880s.

5.   A. 1866

The first women's baseball team was formed at Vassar College in Poughkeepsie, New York.

6.   D. Harry Wright

Wright, a businessman and former cricket player, recruited nine teammates and signed them to contracts with a yearly salary of $950.

QUESTIONS

7. An early rule in baseball allowed players to throw balls at runners off base in order to put them out. What was this practice called?

    A. Socking

    B. Smacking

    C. Soaking

    D. Sinking

8. In what year was the first All-Star Game played?

    A. 1930

    B. 1933

    C. 1935

    D. 1939

9. A women's baseball league, the All-American Girls Professional Baseball League, was formed in what year?

    A. 1940

    B. 1941

    C. 1942

    D. 1943

ANSWERS

7.   C. Soaking

"Soaking" runners was one of the practices prohibited by the Knickerbocker Rules.

8.   B. 1933

The game was held on July 6, 1933, at Comiskey Park in Chicago, and was won by the American League.

9.   D. 1943

The league was formed during World War II, as a way to keep the public interested in the game while many men were fighting in the war. It lasted for 12 seasons, until 1954.

QUESTIONS

10. Player William Arthur "Candy" Cummings is credited with creating what?

    A. The curveball

    B. Batting helmets

    C. Baseball gloves

    D. Cracker Jack

11. What year was the first baseball game broadcast on the radio?

    A. 1920

    B. 1921

    C. 1922

    D. 1923

12. In 1909, sporting goods executive Ben Shibe invented a baseball with what in the center?

    A. Stone

    B. Rubber

    C. Wood

    D. Cork

ANSWERS

10.   A. The curveball

Cummings was the first pitcher to pitch a curveball, which he developed in 1867 while playing with the Brooklyn Excelsiors.

11.   B. 1921

The game, between the Pittsburgh Pirates and the Philadelphia Phillies, was announced by the game's first live play-by-play announcer, Harold Arlin.

12.   D. Cork

Shibe also invented a machine to automatically stitch baseballs. The improvements in the ball gave players much more hitting power.

QUESTIONS

13. Who is credited with creating the Baseball Hall of Fame?
    A. Dale Petroskey
    B. Richard Hanna
    C. Walter Johnson
    D. Stephen Carlton Clark

14. In what year was the first professional baseball game aired on television?
    A. 1939
    B. 1941
    C. 1944
    D. 1948

15. Which pitch, used in the early days of baseball, is now illegal?
    A. Fastball
    B. Knuckleball
    C. Spitball
    D. Curveball

ANSWERS

13.   D. Stephen Carlton Clark

As of 2017, Clark's granddaughter, Jane Forbes Clark, had taken over as the chairman of the board of directors.

14.   A. 1939

The game was a doubleheader played between the Brooklyn Dodgers and the Cincinnati Reds on August 26, 1939.

15.   C. Spitball

The spitball, as the name suggests, was a ball that was altered with the pitcher's saliva, petroleum jelly, tobacco juice, mud, or some other substance, which caused the ball to move in an unpredictable manner.

QUESTIONS

16. Which of the following was never an official league in baseball?
     A. Federal League
     B. New England Association
     C. Players League
     D. Union Association

17. Which baseball team was the first to play with numbers on the backs of their uniforms?
     A. New York Yankees
     B. Cleveland Indians
     C. Boston Red Sox
     D. Chicago Cubs

ANSWERS

16.   B. New England Association

The Union Association and Players League were only active one year each, 1884 and 1890, respectively. The Federal League was active from 1914 to 1915.

17.   B. Cleveland Indians

On opening day in 1929, both the Indians and the New York Yankees were planning to play with numbered uniforms. However, the Yankees game was rained out, so the team wasn't able to show off their new uniforms until the next day.

QUESTIONS

18. True or false:
> The American League is the oldest official league in baseball.

19. True or false:
> The All-American Girls Professional Baseball League played the exact same game as the men who played baseball.

20. True or false:
> The first time the "The Star-Spangled Banner" was sung at a sporting event, it was at a baseball game.

21. True or false:
> A female pitcher once struck out both Babe Ruth and Lou Gehrig.

ANSWERS

18.   False

The National League, which was established in 1876, is the oldest league. The American League wasn't established until 1901.

19.   False

The women played a hybrid baseball/softball game, using a regulation softball and playing on a smaller field. But throughout the years the league was active, the rules of the game continually changed until they almost mirrored professional baseball rules. By their final season, the women were using regulation baseballs and playing on fields only slightly smaller than official Major League Baseball fields.

20.   True

The national anthem, which is now ubiquitous at sporting events throughout the country, was first sung during the middle of the seventh inning of game one of the 1918 World Series.

21.   True

Seventeen-year-old Jackie Mitchell was a minor-league pitcher with the Chattanooga Lookouts. In 1931, the team played an exhibition game against the New York Yankees, and Mitchell struck out both Ruth and Gehrig back-to-back. Rumors have persisted that Mitchell's appearance was a publicity stunt, and the two men struck out on purpose; but Ruth and Gehrig never admitted to such a ploy, and Mitchell, for the rest of her life, insisted that the strikeouts of two of baseball's greatest were genuine.

MASCOTS

1. Which was the first official MLB mascot?
       A. Mr. Red
       B. Phillie Phanatic
       C. Mr. Met
       D. The Oriole Bird

2. What is the name of the mascot of the Toronto Blue Jays?
       A. Ace
       B. Jay
       C. Birdie
       D. Blue

3. Who is the official mascot of the Milwaukee Brewers?
       A. Benny Brewer
       B. Bernie Brewer
       C. Ben the Brewer
       D. Bert Brewer

ANSWERS

1. C. Mr. Met

Mr. Met, the mascot of the New York Mets, is a baseball-headed, Mets-uniform-wearing humanoid who debuted in 1964.

2. A. Ace

Ace is, unsurprisingly, a blue jay. His name comes from the slang term for a team's best starting pitcher.

3. B. Bernie Brewer

Bernie Brewer, a mustached man in lederhosen, has been the team's mascot since 1973.

QUESTIONS

4. The mascot of the Arizona Diamondbacks is D. Baxter the Bobcat. Who created the mascot?

    A. Travis Lee

    B. Matt Williams

    C. Brent Brede

    D. Brantley Bell

5. The mascot of the Miami Marlins is a marlin named what?

    A. Billy

    B. Martin

    C. Bobby

    D. Marty

6. In 2014, the Chicago Cubs introduced a furry, cheerful bear cub as their official mascot. What is his name?

    A. Clive

    B. Clark

    C. Carl

    D. Charlie

ANSWERS

4.   D. Brantley Bell

Bell is the son of Jay Bell, who was a shortstop during the Diamondback's inaugural season.

5.   A. Billy

The Marlin's original team owner, Wayne Huizenga, chose the name because it was different than other "baseball-based" mascot names, and it was easy for young fans to remember.

6.   B. Clark

Clark is named after the location of Wrigley Field, which is at the corner of Clark Street and Addison Street in Chicago.

QUESTIONS

7. The mascot of the St. Louis Cardinals is a cardinal named what?

     A. Fredbird
     B. Freebird
     C. Louis
     D. Loubird

8. The Cincinnati Reds have four official mascots: Mr. Red, Mr. Redlegs, Gapper, and who?

     A. Mrs. Red
     B. Cindy Red
     C. Rosie Red
     D. Redhat

9. What is the name of the Atlanta Braves mascot?

     A. A.B.
     B. Slugger
     C. Ben Brave
     D. Homer

ANSWERS

7.   A. Fredbird

Fredbird's name is play off "redbird," which is a synonym for the cardinal bird. He made his debut in 1979.

8.   C. Rosie Red

Rosie Red is named after a women's committee that formed in the 1960s when a lack of interest in the baseball team almost compelled it to move to another city. The women, who created a group called Rooters Organized to Stimulate Interest and Enthusiasm in the Cincinnati Reds, managed to stir up enough fan excitement to keep the team in their hometown. Rosie Red has been cheering for the Reds ever since!

9.   D. Homer

Homer is a humanoid with a baseball head, not unlike Mr. Met and Mr. Red. His full name is "Homer the Brave," a play on the final line of the national anthem. And "homer," of course, is slang for a home run!

QUESTIONS

10. What year did the Baltimore Orioles debut their mascot, the Oriole Bird?
- A. 1967
- B. 1970
- C. 1975
- D. 1979

11. The mascot of the Detroit Tigers is named what?
- A. Paws
- B. Claws
- C. Roar
- D. Stripes

12. The mascot for the Philadelphia Phillies is the Phillie Phanatic. According to his "official bio," where is the Phillie Phanatic originally from?
- A. The moon
- B. The Galapagos Islands
- C. Tasmania
- D. Guam

ANSWERS

10.   D. 1979

Orioles players wore a cartoon version of an oriole bird on their uniforms from 1966 to 1988, and in 1979 they transformed it into a live-action mascot. From 1989 to 2011, players sported a more lifelike depiction of an oriole on their uniforms; but in 2012, they went back to the cartoon version, which matches the Oriole Bird mascot.

11.   A. Paws

Paws is a tiger who made his first appearance during the 1995 season.

12.   B. The Galapagos Islands

The Phillie Phanatic, a furry green biped with purple eyelashes and blue eyebrows, is considered one of the most recognizable mascots in American sports.

QUESTIONS

13. The official mascot of the Pittsburgh Pirates is the Pirate Parrot, who debuted in what year?

    A. 1979

    B. 1980

    C. 1981

    D. 1982

14. What is the name of the Texas Rangers mascot?

    A. Tex

    B. Captain Ranger

    C. Rangers Captain

    D. Big R

15. The mascot of the Kansas City Royals is named Sluggerrr (with three R's!). What type of animal is he?

    A. Dog

    B. Lion

    C. Rhinoceros

    D. Zebra

ANSWERS

13.   A. 1979

The Pirate Parrot is based on the tradition of pirates carrying pet parrots on their shoulders, such as in the book Treasure Island *by Robert Louis Stevenson.*

14.   C. Rangers Captain

Rangers Captain is a palomino horse who wears a uniform featuring number 72, in honor of the year the team first played in Arlington, Texas.

15.   B. Lion

Instead of a lion's mane, Sluggerrr has a crown on top of his head.

QUESTIONS

16. The Oakland Athletics introduced an elephant mascot in 1997. What is his name?
>A. Trunk
>B. Stomper
>C. Elly
>D. Olly

17. The official mascot of the San Diego Padres is the "swinging" what?
>A. Friar
>B. Monk
>C. Nun
>D. Priest

18. The Minnesota Twins mascot is a bear named T.C. Bear. What do his initials stand for?
>A. Team Club
>B. Twin Cities
>C. Total Catch
>D. Two Cities

ANSWERS

16.   B. Stomper

In the early days of the franchise, rivals of the A's referred to the new team as a "white elephant." Oakland management decided to take the insult and turn it into a symbol for the new team!

17.   A. Friar

The Swinging Friar was a mascot for the Padres when they were still a minor-league team, as far back as 1958. When they joined the MLB in 1969, the team held on to the baseball-loving friar as its mascot.

18.   B. Twin Cities

T.C., who made his debut in 2000, is named after the "Twin Cities" of Minneapolis and St. Paul.

QUESTIONS

19. The secondary mascot of the Arizona Diamondbacks is the D-backs Luchador. What is a luchador?
  A. A wrestler
  B. A singer
  C. A bull fighter
  D. A baker

20. In addition to the Pirate Parrot, the Pittsburgh Pirates also feature what group of mascots?
  A. The Pizzas
  B. The Pierogis
  C. The Knishes
  D. The Kolaches

21. Like the Pirates, the Milwaukee Brewers also feature a culinary race during games. What food is featured?
  A. French fries
  B. Cheese
  C. Sausages
  D. Cookies

ANSWERS

19.   A. A wrestler

Luchadors are popular professional wrestlers in Mexico. The D-backs Luchador was introduced to represent the team's Hispanic fans, and he wears a black cape, red pants, and a mask patterned after the team's logo.

20.   B. The Pierogis

The Pierogis are a group of six people dressed in pierogi costumes who race between innings at Pirates games. The Pierogis include Jalapeno Hannah, Cheese Chester, Sauerkraut Saul, Oliver Onion, Bacon Burt, and Potato Pete.

21.   C. Sausages

The Sausages made their first appearance in the 1990s, and included a German bratwurst, a Polish Kielbasa, and an Italian sausage. A hot dog and Spanish chorizo were later added to the lineup.

QUESTIONS

22. True or false:

Only two teams in Major League Baseball don't have official mascots.

23. True or false:

In addition to Wally the Green Monster, the Boston Red Sox have two other mascots called Lefty and Righty.

24. True or false:

In the 1970s, the Milwaukee Brewers featured a female counterpart mascot to Bernie Brewer named Bonnie Brewer.

25. True or false:

The New York Yankees have never had an official mascot.

ANSWERS

22.   False

There are three teams that don't have official mascots: The New York Yankees, the Los Angeles Dodgers, and the Los Angeles Angels of Anaheim.

23.   True

Lefty and Righty are giant red socks who wear ballcaps. They usually make appearances at large events and on weekend afternoon games at Fenway Park.

24.   True

Bonnie Brewer, a young blond woman who wore a gold shirt and blue lederhosen, was known for carrying a broom during the seventh-inning stretch to "sweep" the bases. Although she was discontinued after 1979, Bonnie still makes occasional appearances during the Brewers' "Retro Fridays" promotions at Miller Park.

25.   False

Between 1979 and 1981, the Yankees had a mascot named "Dandy." Dandy, a large, pinstriped bird with a Yankees cap, was created by the same team that created the Phillie Phanatic. His use was leased to the team for three years, but fan interest was low and Yankees management showed lackluster support for the mascot. After the three-year lease was up, Dandy was retired.

MANAGERS

....

1. Which former player was the longest-serving manager in Major League Baseball history?

     A. Bobby Cox

     B. Tony La Russa

     C. Connie Mack

     D. Casey Stengel

2. Which manger holds the record for the highest win percentage, at .615?

     A. Casey Stengel

     B. Joe Torre

     C. Lou Piniella

     D. Joe McCarthy

3. In what year did the MLB create the Manager of the Year award?

     A. 1954

     B. 1970

     C. 1983

     D. 1988

ANSWERS

1.   **C. Connie Mack**

Mack, a catcher for the Washington Nationals, Buffalo Bisons, and Pittsburgh Pirates, began his managerial career with the Pirates in 1894. In 1901, he joined the new Philadelphia Athletics (now the Oakland Athletics), and managed the club for an impressive 50 seasons!

2.   **D. Joe McCarthy**

Between 1926 and 1950, McCarthy managed the Chicago Cubs, New York Yankees, and Boston Red Sox. Over the course of his career, he managed 3,487 games, winning 2,125.

3.   **C. 1983**

The 30 members of the Baseball Writers Association of America vote on the winners in both the American and National leagues each year.

QUESTIONS

4. Connie Mack spent a remarkable 50 seasons managing the Philadelphia Athletics. Who took the reins after he left?

    A. Jimmy Dykes

    B. John McGraw

    C. Bucky Harris

    D. Bill Rigney

5. Who was the first American League manager to win the Manager of the Year award?

    A. Terry Francona

    B. John McNamara

    C. Tony La Russa

    D. Lou Piniella

6. Which manager led the Philadelphia Phillies to their first World Series win in 1980?

    A. Buck Showalter

    B. Dallas Green

    C. Mike Scioscia

    D. Davey Johnson

ANSWERS

4.   A. Jimmy Dykes

Dykes was a former second and third baseman for the Athletics, and had been one of Mack's most valuable players.

5.   C. Tony La Russa

La Russa won the award when he was managing the Chicago White Sox, who won the AL West in 1983.

6.   B. Dallas Green

Green's managerial career spanned from 1979 to 1996. In addition to the Phillies, he also managed the New York Yankees and the New York Mets.

QUESTIONS

7. The first official World Series was played between the Boston Americans, managed by Jimmy Collins, and the Pittsburgh Pirates, managed by whom?

      A. Bill Watkins

      B. Connie Mack

      C. Honus Wagner

      D. Fred Clarke

8. Who was the first National League manager to win the Manager of the Year award?

      A. Bobby Cox

      B. Tommy Lasorda

      C. Lou Piniella

      D. Jim Leyland

9. What former Yankee was the manager of the Cincinnati Reds when they won their last World Series title in 1990?

      A. Lou Piniella

      B. Yogi Berra

      C. Don Mattingly

      D. Hal Lanier

ANSWERS

7.   D. Fred Clarke

Clarke simultaneously played for and managed the Pirates for fifteen years, leading the team to four National League pennants and a World Series title in 1909.

8.   B. Tommy Lasorda

Lasorda managed the Los Angeles Dodgers from 1976 to 1996, and was inducted into the Baseball Hall of Fame in 1997.

9.   A. Lou Piniella

Left fielder Piniella helped the Yankees win two World Series titles, in 1977 and 1978. He is a three-time Manager of the Year winner: 1995 and 2001 with the Seattle Mariners, and 2008 with the Chicago Cubs.

QUESTIONS

10. Manager Alan Trammell had the unfortunate distinction of leading the Detroit Tigers during their worst season ever, when they lost 119 games. Before he managed the team, Trammell played what position on the Tigers?

    A. First base
    B. Shortstop
    C. Right field
    D. Catcher

11. Who was the first manager to be ejected from a game before it even started?

    A. Earl Weaver
    B. Bobby Cox
    C. Billy Martin
    D. Lou Piniella

12. Which team was former player Bobby Valentine managing in 2000?

    A. Baltimore Orioles
    B. New York Mets
    C. Pittsburgh Pirates
    D. Cincinnati Reds

ANSWERS

10.   B. Shortstop

Trammell's entire 19-year playing career was as shortstop for the Detroit Tigers, from 1977 to 1996.

11.   A. Earl Weaver

Weaver managed the Baltimore Orioles between 1968 and 1986. In the middle of a game in 1969, he was ejected for smoking a cigarette in the dugout. Unhappy with the call, Weaver decided to mock the umpire's decision the next day by delivering his lineup card to the umpiring crew with a candy cigarette in his mouth. They were unamused, and Weaver was ejected from the game before a single inning of play!

12.   B. New York Mets

Valentine led the Mets to a National League Championship that year, but the team was defeated in the World Series (dubbed the "Subway Series") by their crosstown rivals, the New York Yankees.

QUESTIONS

13. Who was the first manager to win a Manager of the Year award for both the American League and the National League?

    A. Tony La Russa
    B. Lou Piniella
    C. Jim Leyland
    D. Bobby Cox

14. Which manager holds the record for most losses, at 3,948?

    A. John McGraw
    B. Connie Mack
    C. Tony La Russa
    D. Bobby Cox

15. Who managed the Texas Rangers in 1972, the first year the team played in Texas?

    A. Ted Williams
    B. Jim Lemon
    C. Gil Hodges
    D. Eddie Yost

ANSWERS

13.   D. Bobby Cox

In 1985, Cox won the award when he was managing the AL Toronto Blue Jays. He later won again in 1991, managing the NL Atlanta Braves.

14.   B. Connie Mack

Mack managed an amazing 7,755 games during his career, and also holds the record for most wins at 3,731.

15.   A. Ted Williams

The Red Sox great began managing the team in 1969, when they were still the Washington Senators.

QUESTIONS

16. Gil Hodges was the manager of which team in 1969?
    A. New York Mets
    B. New York Yankees
    C. Baltimore Orioles
    D. Boston Red Sox

17. Former second baseman Joe Gordon helmed which team during its inaugural season?
    A. Texas Rangers
    B. Kansas City Royals
    C. Seattle Mariners
    D. Houston Astros

18. Former second baseman Kid Gleason managed which team from 1919 to 1923?
    A. New York Yankees
    B. Chicago White Sox
    C. Cleveland Indians
    D. Pittsburgh Pirates

ANSWERS

16.   A. New York Mets

The former first baseman led the Mets to their first World Series win in 1969 over the heavily favored Baltimore Orioles, leading to the team's nickname, the "Miracle Mets."

17.   B. Kansas City Royals

Gordon was a nine-time All Star and five-time World Series champion who played for the New York Yankees and the Cleveland Indians before beginning his managerial career.

18.   B. Chicago White Sox

Gleason managed the team throughout the infamous "Black Sox" scandal of 1919, but since he was not involved in the players' plot to throw the World Series, he went on to manage the team for four more seasons.

QUESTIONS

19. True or false:

After the New York Yankees lost the 1964 World Series to the St. Louis Cardinals, they fired their manager and hired the Cardinals manager.

20. True or false:

Tony La Russa once stated that Albert Pujols was the best player he ever managed.

21. True or false:

Manager Billy Martin helmed the New York Yankees four separate times.

ANSWERS

19.   True

The Yankees fired then-manager Yogi Berra, and replaced him with Johnny Keane, who led the Cardinals to their series win. Unfortunately, the move backfired, as the Yankees finished in 6th place the next year, and Keane was fired in 1966.

20.   True

In fact, La Russa praised Pujols several times during his career, saying "if he's healthy, there will be no better hitter" and "I've never seen anyone quite like him."

21.   False

Martin had quite the on/off relationship with the Yankees, managing them a total of five separate times: 1975-1978, 1979, 1983, 1985, and 1988. At the time of his accidental death in 1989, Martin was preparing to manage the Yankees for a sixth time.

ON THE SIDELINES:
UMPIRES AND ANNOUNCERS

1. What was the name of the first official umpire in Major League Baseball?
- A. Bill Klem
- B. Hank O'Day
- C. Billy McLean
- D. Cy Rigler

2. Which announcer provided play-by-play for the Atlanta Braves for 33 years?
- A. Skip Caray
- B. Russ Hodges
- C. Milo Hamilton
- D. Bob Prince

3. The "ready" position assumed by umpires prior to each play is known by what abbreviation?
- A. HOHS
- B. HOKS
- C. HSKT
- D. HOKG

ANSWERS

1.   C. Billy McLean

McLean was the umpire for the first official National League game on April 22, 1876. He continued to umpire until 1890.

2.   A. Skip Caray

Caray, son of legendary announcer Harry Caray, began announcing for the Braves in 1976. Sadly, he passed away in 2008, just three days after calling his last game.

3.   B. HOKS

"HOKS" stands for "hands on knees set," and refers to the stance taken by umpires right before a ball is pitched.

QUESTIONS

4. The first recipients of the Ford C. Frick award were former New York Yankees announcer Red Barber and who else?

    A. Mel Allen
    B. Vin Scully
    C. Bob Elson
    D. Curt Gowdy

5. Who broke the race barrier and became the first African-American umpire in Major League Baseball?

    A. Emmett Ashford
    B. Joe West
    C. Ernie Quigley
    D. Bill Summers

6. Who was the recipient of the Ford C. Frick award in 2017?

    A. Jim Powell
    B. Joe Davis
    C. Tom Cheek
    D. Bill King

ANSWERS

4. A. Mel Allen

Allen also announced for the New York Yankees, mostly in the '40s, '50s, and '60s. His broadcasts were familiar to millions of listeners, and he became known as "the Voice of the Yankees."

5. A. Emmett Ashford

It wasn't until 1966 that Ashford became an umpire with the American League. He worked until 1970, umpiring all five games of the 1970 World Series.

6. D. Bill King

King began his broadcasting career during World War II, when he was stationed on the island of Guam. By 1958, he was announcing for the San Francisco Giants, and later, he became the voice of the Oakland Athletics. He worked for the A's for 25 years, from 1981 to 2005, and is the longest-tenured A's announcer in the franchise's history.

QUESTIONS

7. What colorful nickname is sometimes used to refer to an umpire?
     A. Red
     B. Blue
     C. White
     D. Green

8. Who was the play-by-play announcer for the Philadelphia Phillies from 1971 until 2009?
     A. Ernie Harwell
     B. Bob Prince
     C. Harry Kalas
     D. Chuck Thompson

9. Who was the first woman to work as an umpire in professional baseball?
     A. Bernice Gera
     B. Pam Postema
     C. Amanda Clement
     D. Ria Cortesio

ANSWERS

7. B. Blue

Umpires have traditionally worn blue-colored outfits, leading to the nickname. Not all umpires appreciate the moniker, however, and prefer to simply be called by name!

8. C. Harry Kalas

Kalas began his career with the Houston Astros in 1965. He was then hired by the Phillies, where he called the first and last games at Veterans Stadium, and the first game at Citizens Bank Park.

9. A. Bernice Gera

Gera graduated from the Florida Baseball School in 1967. She was initially denied a position by the National Association of Baseball Leagues (NABL), who claimed she lacked the physical requirements for the job. But Gera took the NABL to court, eventually winning the right to work with the New York-Penn League. She umpired her first professional game in 1972.

QUESTIONS

10. Which announcer was fired from the Detroit Tigers in 1991, only to later be rehired due to his popularity?

    A. Ernie Harwell

    B. Lindsey Nelson

    C. Chuck Thompson

    D. Bob Murphy

11. In what year did MLB begin using instant replay for umpires to review disputed plays?

    A. 2005

    B. 2006

    C. 2007

    D. 2008

12. Joe Garagiola was known for his nearly 30-year career with NBC television, broadcasting baseball games. But before he became an announcer, he played nine seasons in MLB at what position?

    A. First base

    B. Catcher

    C. Left field

    D. Third base

ANSWERS

10. A. Ernie Harwell

Harwell was let go when radio station WJR decided to "go in a new direction." But fans were outraged by the decision, and Harwell returned to the station part-time in 1993. He resumed his full-time announcing duties in 1999, and worked until his retirement in 2002.

11. D. 2008

Major League Baseball was late to adopt the technology, as it had already been in use for football, basketball, and hockey. When it was first introduced to MLB, it was only used to uphold or overturn home run calls; but the rules and regulations governing its use have been tweaked several times since its implementation.

12. B. Catcher

The former catcher, who played with the Cardinals, Pirates, Cubs, and Giants, went on to call three All-Star Games, three National League Championships, and three World Series. He also announced games for the New York Yankees from 1965 to 1967, when he had the chance to call Mickey Mantle's 500th home run.

QUESTIONS

13. Which Seattle Mariners announcer was the recipient of the Ford C. Frick award in 2008?
 A. Dave Sims
 B. Gary Hill
 C. Dave Niehaus
 D. Dan Wilson

14. Which broadcaster announced the first MLB game on television in 1939?
 A. Red Barber
 B. Mel Allen
 C. Bob Elson
 D. Russ Hodges

15. Approximately how many total umpires work in the Major League?
 A. 120
 B. 112
 C. 90
 D. 70

ANSWERS

13.   C. Dave Niehaus

Niehaus broadcast for the Mariners from their first season in 1977 until his death in 2010. He was the first announcer to dub player Alex Rodriguez "A-Rod," and he was known for his catchphrase, "my, oh my!"

14.   A. Red Barber

Over his four-decade career, Barber announced for the Cincinnati Reds, Brooklyn Dodgers, and New York Yankees.

15.   D. 70

There are about 70 umpires in MLB, and 225 in the minor leagues. Umpires must work their way up through the minors before they get a shot at the coveted MLB.

QUESTIONS

16. Jack Brickhouse was a play-by-play announcer for which team until 1981?
  A. Chicago Cubs
  B. Oakland Athletics
  C. Cleveland Indians
  D. Detroit Tigers

17. What is the name for the most senior or experienced umpire in a game?
  A. Head umpire
  B. Captain
  C. Crew chief
  D. Field foreman

18. Which legendary announcer did Reggie Jackson nickname "The Voice of God"?
  A. Phil Rizzuto
  B. Bob Sheppard
  C. Vin Scully
  D. Harry Caray

ANSWERS

16.   A. Chicago Cubs

Brickhouse covered Cubs games on WGN-TV from 1948 to 1981. He was given the Ford C. Frick award in 1983 and was inducted into the American Sportscasters Association Hall of Fame in 1985.

17.   C. Crew chief

The crew chief acts as supervisor, assuring that the rest of the umpire crew follows the rules and regulations of the Office of the Commissioner.

18.   B. Bob Sheppard

Sheppard was the public address announcer at Yankee Stadium for 56 years, where he announced more than 4,500 games. Beloved by fans and players alike, he announced well into his 90s, and didn't officially retire until he was 99 years old. Before Sheppard retired, Yankees shortstop Derek Jeter asked him to record his introduction. Sheppard passed away in 2010, but Jeter continued to use the recording of the announcer's voice until his final game at Yankee Stadium on September 25, 2014.

QUESTIONS

19. True or false:
> No woman has ever umpired an MLB regular
> season game.

20. True or false:
> Announcer Vin Scully spent more years with
> the Dodgers than anyone else associated with the
> organization.

21. True or false:
> In 1996, an umpire died on Opening Day, after calling
> for a time out in the first inning and collapsing on
> the field.

22. True or false:
> Umpires do not allow any kind of foreign substance to
> be applied to baseballs used in MLB games.

ANSWERS

19.   True

Although several women, including Pam Postema and Ria Cortesio, have umpired spring training and exhibition games, no woman has yet had the chance to umpire a regular season game.

20.   False

Scully is just one year shy of Tommy Lasorda's record-breaking 68 years with the Dodgers, as player, manager, and executive.

21.   True

Sadly, in 1996 umpire John McSherry suffered a massive heart attack while working at home plate during the Cincinnati Reds Opening Day game against the Montreal Expos. He died within the hour, and the game was postponed, as shocked umpires and players grieved for their colleague.

22.   False

Actually, umpires deliberately rub baseballs with mud before they are used for play. But not just any mud: the prepackaged mud is called "Lena Blackburn Original Baseball Rubbing Mud," and it is collected from a location near the Delaware River in New Jersey. The mud has been used by the Major League since the 1950s, to make brand new baseballs less slick and easier to handle. Just one of baseball's dirty little secrets!

PITCHING GREATS

1. Who was the first pitcher to win 24 games in a season before he reached 21 years of age?

    A. Sandy Koufax

    B. Bob Gibson

    C. Bob Feller

    D. Walter Johnson

2. In 1948, which pitcher became the oldest man to ever debut in MLB, at 42 years old?

    A. Mort Cooper

    B. Satchel Paige

    C. Bucky Walters

    D. Bob Feller

3. People remember Babe Ruth as a slugger, but he started his career as a pitcher. In his best year as a pitcher, 1916, how many wins did he have?

    A. 19

    B. 21

    C. 23

    D. 25

ANSWERS

1.   C. Bob Feller

Feller began playing for the Cleveland Indians in 1936, when he was only 17 years old. He earned 24 wins in the 1939 season, just before he turned 21.

2.   B. Satchel Paige

Paige had been playing professionally since he was 20 years old, but because of segregation, he was forced to play only with Negro League baseball. When the sport was integrated in the late '40s, Paige, along with trailblazers like Jackie Robinson and Larry Doby, was finally able to join MLB.

3.   C. 23

Ruth had 23 wins and 12 losses with the Boston Red Sox, logging 170 strikeouts and an ERA of 1.75.

QUESTIONS

4. Three-time NL Cy Young Award winner Tom Seaver was known by what nickname?

      A. Super Seaver

      B. King Tom

      C. Tom Terrific

      D. Seaver Superb

5. While playing for the New York Yankees, Jim Abbott pitched a no-hitter on September 4, 1993. What made his achievement especially remarkable?

      A. He used to be a catcher

      B. It was his second no-hitter in a row

      C. It was his very first game

      D. He only has one hand

6. Which pitcher was known by the nicknames "Big Six," "The Christian Gentleman," and "The Gentleman's Hurler"?

      A. Christy Mathewson

      B. Walter Johnson

      C. Warren Spahn

      D. Tommy John

ANSWERS

4.   **C. Tom Terrific**

Seaver joined the New York Mets in 1967, when the team was in last place. He was a key part of the team's amazing turnaround in 1969, when the "Miracle Mets" won the World Series.

5.   **D. He only has one hand**

Abbott was born without a right hand, but it didn't stop him from spending 11 seasons in the major leagues. He logged 888 strikeouts during his career, and he helped Team U.S.A. win the gold at the 1988 Olympic Games in Seoul, Korea.

6.   **A. Christy Mathewson**

Playing in the early days of the game, Mathewson was unusual not only for his six-foot height (a rarity during the era), but also for his devout, religious ways. While most baseball players had reputations as gamblers, drinkers, and womanizers, Mathewson eschewed such a lifestyle, and even refrained from playing games on Sundays.

QUESTIONS

7. Who threw 17 strikeouts during game one of the 1968 World Series?

    A. Mickey Lolich

    B. Denny McLain

    C. Bob Gibson

    D. Ray Washburn

8. Roger Clemens was the first pitcher in history to strike out how many batters in a nine-inning game?

    A. 17

    B. 18

    C. 19

    D. 20

9. Who is the only pitcher in MLB history to win at least 15 games per season for 17 straight seasons?

    A. Greg Maddux

    B. Nolan Ryan

    C. Roger Clemens

    D. Randy Johnson

ANSWERS

7.   C. Bob Gibson

Gibson, who played 17 seasons with the St. Louis Cardinals, also recorded an amazing 1.12 ERA during the 1968 regular season. Although St. Louis would go on to lose the 1968 series, they won in 1964 and 1967, both times naming Gibson MVP.

8.   D. 20

Clemens, pitching for the Boston Red Sox, performed the feat against the Seattle Mariners on April 29, 1986. Ten years later, he later repeated the accomplishment in a game against the Detroit Tigers.

9.   A. Greg Maddux

Maddux, who pitched from 1986 to 2008, won more games during the 1990s than any other pitcher. Throughout his career, he logged an impressive 355 wins and 3,371 strikeouts.

QUESTIONS

10. Pitcher Grover Cleveland Alexander, who played from 1911 to 1930 with the Phillies, Cubs, and Cardinals, was once portrayed in a biographical film called *The Winning Team* by which actor?

    A. Tony Curtis
    B. Cary Grant
    C. Ronald Reagan
    D. Elvis Presley

11. What is the full name of Cy Young Award winner CC Sabathia?

    A. Carsten Charles
    B. Carlos Cameron
    C. Connor Christian
    D. Christopher Cody

12. Who was the first pitcher to win four Cy Young Awards during his career?

    A. Curt Schilling
    B. John Smoltz
    C. Steve Carlton
    D. Greg Maddux

ANSWERS

10. **C. Ronald Reagan**

Yes, the baseball player—who was born during the first term of President Grover Cleveland and named accordingly—was portrayed by an actor who would later become president!

11. **A. Carsten Charles**

Carsten Charles Sabathia Jr. won the Cy Young Award in 2007 while playing with the Cleveland Indians, becoming the second Cleveland pitcher, after Gaylord Perry, to win the award.

12. **C. Steve Carlton**

Carlton's career spanned from 1965 to 1988, where he earned the fourth-most strikeouts of all MLB pitchers. In addition to the Cy Young Award, Carlton was also a 10-time All Star, two-time World Series Champion, and a Gold Glove Award winner. His number on the Philadelphia Phillies—32—was retired in 1989.

QUESTIONS

13. As of the end of the 2016 season, who was the last pitcher to pitch a perfect game?

A. Randy Johnson
B. Felix Hernandez
C. Jake Arrieta
D. Johan Santana

14. Which pitcher won more games than any other during the 1960s?

A. Juan Marichal
B. Bob Gibson
C. Don Drysdale
D. Sandy Koufax

15. As of 2016, who is the only pitcher to have his number retired by the New York Mets?

A. David Cone
B. Tom Seaver
C. Al Leiter
D. Dwight Gooden

ANSWERS

13.   B. Felix Hernandez

Hernandez, playing for the Seattle Mariners, pitched a rare perfect game against the Tampa Bay Rays on August 15, 2012.

14.   A. Juan Marichal

Marichal played for the San Francisco Giants from 1960 to 1973, and then the Boston Red Sox and Los Angeles Dodgers for the last two seasons of his career. He retired with 243 wins and 2,303 strikeouts.

15.   B. Tom Seaver

Although Seaver played for three other teams—the Cincinnati Reds, Chicago White Sox, and Boston Red Sox—he is best remembered as number 41 on the New York Mets. He is still the Mets' all-time leader in wins.

QUESTIONS

16. Which of the following imposing pitchers never won the Cy Young Award?
A. Johan Santana
B. Nolan Ryan
C. Barry Zito
D. Roy Halladay

17. What year was dubbed "the year of the pitcher" in MLB history?
A. 1968
B. 1972
C. 1988
D. 1991

18. Who holds the record for the most games won by a left-handed pitcher?
A. Sandy Koufax
B. Clayton Kershaw
C. Randy Johnson
D. Warren Spahn

ANSWERS

16.   **B. Nolan Ryan**

Incredibly, although Ryan pitched a record seven no-hitters, logged 5,714 strikeouts, and won 324 games, he was never honored with a Cy Young Award!

17.   **A. 1968**

Pitching dominated games throughout 1968, with the average score of a game being a low-run 4 to 2. And the score of that year's All Star Game? 1 to 0!

18.   **D. Warren Spahn**

Spahn logged 363 wins throughout his 21-year career. In 1999, the Warren Spahn Award was introduced by the Oklahoma Sports Hall of Fame, and is given each year to the best left-handed pitcher in MLB.

QUESTIONS

19. What is the most common score on which a perfect game ends?

      A. 1-0

      B. 2-0

      C. 3-0

      D. 4-0

20. Which poor pitcher holds the record for most career losses without ever notching a win?

      A. Bill Greif

      B. Jason Bere

      C. Milt Gaston

      D. Terry Felton

21. What is the record for the most strikeouts in a single game?

      A. 20

      B. 21

      C. 22

      D. 23

ANSWERS

19.   A. 1-0

Seven of the 23 perfect games in history have ended with a score of 1-0, more than any other perfect game score. The next most common score is 4-0, with five games ending that way.

20.   D. Terry Felton

Felton pitched for the Minnesota Twins from 1979 to 1982, with a record of zero wins and 16 losses. After he was released by the Twins, he moved on to a different career and became a Captain in the East Baton Rouge Parish Sherriff's Office.

21.   B. 21

The feat was accomplished by Washington Senator pitcher Tom Cheney, who struck out 21 batters in a 16-inning game against the Baltimore Orioles in 1962. Lucky for Cheney, the Senators finally won the game 2-1!

QUESTIONS

22. True or false:

Satchel Paige was not only one of the oldest men to ever debut in MLB, but he retired as the oldest player ever in the majors.

23. True or false:

No pitcher has ever thrown more than one perfect game.

24. True or false:

New York Mets pitcher Tom Seaver once struck out eleven batters in a row.

25. True or false:

An anonymous bidder bought a sock with Boston Red Sox pitcher Curt Schilling's blood on it for more than $90,000.

ANSWERS

22.   True

Paige retired in 1965 at the age of 59, retiring nine out of the ten batters he faced in his last MLB appearance. In 1971 he became the first African-American to be inducted into the National Baseball Hall of Fame, and he is still considered one of the greatest pitchers in history.

23.   True

Perfect games—when a pitcher doesn't allow a single runner to reach base—are so rare that only 23 perfect games have ever been pitched in the history of MLB. And no pitcher has ever accomplished the feat more than once.

24.   False

Seaver "only" struck out ten batters in a row, in a game against the San Diego Padres on April 22, 1970. He struck out 19 batters total during the game, which the Mets won 2-1.

25.   True

During the 2004 postseason, Schilling played with an injury. He repeatedly needed a minor surgical procedure to stabilize a tendon in his ankle, and his movement when pitching resulted in torn sutures. He famously won game 6 of the ALCS against the New York Yankees wearing a blood-soaked sock, which later went up for auction and was bought for $92,613 by an anonymous bidder!

ODDS AND ENDS

1. When was baseball officially added as a sport in the Olympics?
   A. 1904
   B. 1946
   C. 1980
   D. 1992

2. Which "corn"-y expression refers to an easy fly ball?
   A. Can of corn
   B. Cornhusk
   C. Corncob
   D. Popcorn

3. The Atlanta Braves began in 1871 as what team?
   A. Philadelphia Athletics
   B. Boston Red Stockings
   C. Washington Olympics
   D. Chicago White Stockings

ANSWERS

1.   D. 1992

Baseball was played in the Summer Olympics from 1992 until 2008. The sport was then voted out of the games, but in 2016, the International Olympic Committee decided to bring the sport back for the 2020 game in Tokyo.

2.   A. Can of corn

The expression originated from the way old-time grocers would use their aprons to catch cans knocked off shelves.

3.   B. Boston Red Stockings

Before adopting the Braves name, the team was also known as the Red Caps, the Beaneaters, the Doves, the Rustlers, and the Bees.

QUESTIONS

4. The first five men inducted into the Baseball Hall of Fame in Cooperstown were Ty Cobb, Babe Ruth, Christy Mathewson, Walter Johnson, and who?

    A. Honus Wagner
    B. Cy Young
    C. Tris Speaker
    D. Connie Mack

5. How old was the youngest player to ever pitch in a Major League game?

    A. 15
    B. 16
    C. 17
    D. 18

6. Center fielder Rick Monday is best known for what non-baseball feat?

    A. Running a marathon
    B. Building his own house
    C. Performing CPR on a fan
    D. Saving an American flag

ANSWERS

4.   A. Honus Wagner

The shortstop logged 3,430 hits, 101 home runs, 1,732 RBIs, and 722 stolen bases over his career, with a batting average of .329.

5.   A. 15

Fifteen-year-old Joe Nuxhall pitched 2/3 of an inning for the Cincinnati Reds on June 10, 1944. The unusual pitching decision was the result of player shortages during World War II. Nuxhall eventually rejoined the Reds at the ripe old age of 24!

6.   D. Saving an American flag

On April 25, 1976, two protestors ran onto the field at Dodgers Stadium and attempted to set an American flag on fire. Monday, playing for the Chicago Cubs, saw the incident unfolding and ran toward the protestors. He grabbed the flag as the stadium erupted in cheers. The protestors—a father and his 11-year-old son—were escorted from the field, and the father was charged with trespassing. The Dodgers later presented Monday with the flag he saved, and he still considers it a prized possession.

QUESTIONS

7. Which Philadelphia Phillies player had the bad luck of hitting two foul balls in a row that hit the same woman at a game in 1957?

     A. Ed Bouchee

     B. Harry Anderson

     C. Willie Jones

     D. Richie Ashburn

8. Who was the Commissioner of Baseball when Pete Rose was banned from the sport?

     A. Bud Selig

     B. A. Bartlett Giamatti

     C. Fay Vincent

     D. Peter Ueberroth

9. Three-time World Series champion pitcher Curt Schilling hails from which state?

     A. Florida

     B. Montana

     C. Alaska

     D. North Carolina

ANSWERS

7.   D. Richie Ashburn

Ashburn's first foul ball hit Alice Roth (who was the wife of Philadelphia Bulletin sportswriter Earl Roth) and broke the poor spectator's nose. As Roth was being carried off on a stretcher, Ashburn hit a second foul ball that hit Roth again! The two made the most of a bad situation, and struck up a years-long friendship after the unfortunate incident.

8.   B. A. Bartlett Giamatti

Giamatti, a former president of Yale University, was the father of award-winning actor Paul Giamatti.

9.   C. Alaska

The state is rarely scouted by the MLB, and so far, only 11 players in the Major League have been from Alaska.

QUESTIONS

10. Which state is home to the largest baseball bat in the world?

    A. Kentucky

    B. Texas

    C. California

    D. Maryland

11. While the "World" Series is mostly an American event (with occasional appearances by the Toronto Blue Jays), the Baseball World Cup was an international tournament that was held 38 times between 1938 and 2011. How many times did the United States win the tournament?

    A. One

    B. Four

    C. Ten

    D. Sixteen

12. Which of the following players did NOT reach 3,000 hits?

    A. Barry Bonds

    B. Mickey Mantle

    C. Babe Ruth

    D. All of the above

ANSWERS

10.   A. Kentucky

The bat leans against a five-story building in Louisville, Kentucky, which houses the Louisville Slugger Museum and Factory. The giant bat is 120 feet tall and weighs 68,000 pounds.

11.   B. Four

Cuba often dominated the event, scoring 25 total wins. After 2011, the World Baseball Cup was discontinued, but the World Baseball Classic (founded in 2005) has taken its place.

12.   D. All of the above

Surprisingly, none of these baseball greats ever reached 3,000 hits. Neither did Lou Gehrig, Johnny Bench, Alex Rodriguez, or Yogi Berra.

QUESTIONS

13. What deprecating term is sometimes used to refer to the equipment used by catchers?
- A. Idiot apparatus
- B. Tools of ignorance
- C. Fool's gear
- D. Pinhead paraphernalia

14. Who was the tallest player in MLB history?
- A. Chris Young
- B. Michael Pineda
- C. Adam Wainwright
- D. Jon Rauch

15. Which player celebrated his 100th home run by running around the bases backwards?
- A. Mickey Mantle
- B. Jimmy Piersall
- C. Adam Dunn
- D. Ichiro Suzuki

ANSWERS

13.   B. Tools of ignorance

It is sometimes said that only people who are "ignorant" of the job of the catcher would want the position, because it is so difficult. Catchers are prone to knee problems due to their constant crouching, and every year, they are hit by hundreds of wayward baseballs. Many consider it the toughest position in baseball!

14.   D. Jon Rauch

Rauch, a pitcher who played in MLB from 2002 to 2013, was 6 feet, 11 inches tall. He's also the tallest player to ever hit a home run, which he did off Roger Clemens in August 2004.

15.   B. Jimmy Piersall

Piersall played 17 seasons in MLB with the Red Sox, Indians, Senators, Mets, and Angels. The center fielder had a well-publicized struggle with bipolar disorder, which was chronicled in a book, and later a movie, titled Fear Strikes Out.

QUESTIONS

16. In what year were shin guards introduced for catchers?
    A. 1907
    B. 1908
    C. 1909
    D. 1910

17. Which pitcher appeared on an episode of the classic television series *Mister Ed*?
    A. Don Drysdale
    B. Bob Gibson
    C. Sandy Koufax
    D. Juan Marichal

18. Who is the only player who has gotten two hits with two teams in two different cities on the same day?
    A. Joel Youngblood
    B. Lou Whitaker
    C. Robin Yount
    D. Doug Flynn

ANSWERS

16.   A. 1907

The protective gear was popularized by catcher Roger Bresnahan. At first, fans were taken aback by the use of the equipment. In fact, during the first game that Bresnahan used the guards, fans threw debris on the field and umpire Bill Klem called the game for the safety of the players.

17.   C. Sandy Koufax

Koufax, along with teammates Leo Durocher, John Roseboro, Willie Davis, and Moose Skowron, guest starred in a fourth-season episode in which Mister Ed hits a pitch thrown by Koufax. He then trots around the bases, sliding into home plate. To this day, Koufax is the only pitcher to ever give up a run to a talking horse!

18.   A. Joel Youngblood

The outfielder hit a single for the New York Mets in an afternoon game at Wrigley Field against the Chicago Cubs on August 4, 1982. In the middle of the game, Youngblood was traded to the Montreal Expos, and immediately flew to Philadelphia, where his new team was playing.

QUESTIONS

19. Which manager once returned to the dugout in disguise after he was ejected from a game?

    A. Tony La Russa

    B. Billy Martin

    C. Lou Piniella

    D. Bobby Valentine

20. Most baseball stadiums can accommodate around 45,000 fans. But what is the unofficial record for the lowest attendance at an MLB game?

    A. 53

    B. 347

    C. 786

    D. 1043

21. What is the term for a minor league player who achieves a very short stint in the majors before heading back to the minors?

    A. Cup of coffee

    B. Lunch break

    C. Microwave dinner

    D. Fast food

ANSWERS

19.   D. Bobby Valentine

The incident occurred on June 9, 1999, after New York Mets manager Valentine was ejected for arguing with an umpire. He then donned sunglasses and a fake mustache, and snuck back into the dugout. He wasn't fooling anyone, though: he was suspended for two games and fined $5,000 for the stunt.

20.   B. 347

In August 2011, just 347 fans showed up for a game between the Florida Marlins and the Cincinnati Reds. The low attendance was due to the threat of Hurricane Irene, which was on its way to the Sunshine State. "Officially," the attendance was recorded as 22,505, based on the number of tickets sold, but most of those fans stayed home to prepare for the storm!

21.   A. Cup of coffee

A "cup of coffee" player is someone whose tenure in the majors is so short, he only has time to drink a cup of coffee before heading back to the minors.

QUESTIONS

22. True or false:
   During World War II, a grenade was developed to mimic the size and weight of a baseball, so young men who grew up playing the game would know how to throw it.

23. True or false:
   No player has ever died as a result of an injury incurred during an MLB game.

24. True or false:
   Although Ken Griffey Sr. and Ken Griffey Jr. played in MLB at the same time, they never played for the same team.

ANSWERS

22.   True

The "BEANO T-13" hand grenade was a spherical grenade that weighed about 5.5 ounces—the same as a baseball. The designers thought that the familiar size and weight would make it easier for young men to throw the grenade with accuracy. However, the grenade was known to detonate prematurely, resulting in more injuries to Americans than enemy troops, and it was quickly discontinued.

23.   False

On August 16, 1920, Cleveland Indians shortstop Ray Chapman was hit in the head by a pitch thrown by Carl Mays of the New York Yankees. The impact fractured his skull, and he died 12 hours later. The tragic incident was partly responsible for the end of the spitball in baseball: up until this time, pitchers were allowed to rub and scuff the ball with dirt, tobacco juice, sandpaper, or anything else they could get their hands on. The end result was a dirty, misshapen ball that was difficult for batters to see. Many believe that Chapman was unable to see the dirt-colored ball when it was pitched, giving him no time to react to the projectile.

24.   False

The duo became the first father and son to play on the same team in 1990 when they were both on the Seattle Mariners roster. On September 14 of that year, they even hit back-to-back home runs!

STREAKS

1. How many consecutive seasons did left fielder Rickey Henderson steal 40 or more bases?

     A. 8
     B. 11
     C. 14
     D. 15

2. Derek Jeter of the New York Yankees, and who is the other?

     A. Hank Aaron
     B. Ichiro Suzuki
     C. Pete Rose
     D. Barry Bonds

3. New York Yankee Joe DiMaggio had a hitting streak in 1941 that lasted for how many games?

     A. 42
     B. 45
     C. 51
     D. 56

ANSWERS

1.   C. 14

Henderson, who logged 1,406 steals throughout his career, stole 40 or more bases in each season from 1980 through 1993.

2.   A. Hank Aaron

Two players boast 17 consecutive seasons with 150 or more hits. One is Aaron, who played with the Atlanta Braves (originally the Milwaukee Braves), logged at least 150 hits each season from 1955 through 1971. Jeter's streak lasted from the 1996 season through 2012.

3.   D. 56

During the streak, DiMaggio batted .408, with 55 RBIs and 15 home runs. The day after his streak ended, he began another hitting streak of 16 games. Amazingly, he managed to hit in 72 of 73 straight games!

QUESTIONS

4. Which player had a streak of 23 seasons hitting .300 or better?

      A. Ichiro Suzuki
      B. Joe DiMaggio
      C. Hank Aaron
      D. Ty Cobb

5. Ted Williams of the Boston Red Sox managed to reach base in a streak of how many games?

      A. 84
      B. 85
      C. 86
      D. 87

6. What is the unusual name of the player who, in 1893, reached base on 17 consecutive plate appearances?

      A. Bunny Brief
      B. Piggy Ward
      C. Sugar Cain
      D. Possum Whitted

ANSWERS

4.   D. Ty Cobb

Cobb boasts a career batting average of .367—a record he's held since 1928!

5.   A. 84

Williams' streak lasted from July 1 until September 27, 1949.

6.   B. Piggy Ward

Ward's given name was Frank Gray Ward, and he played in the major leagues from 1883 to 1894. During his streak, he had eight hits, eight walks, and was hit by a pitch once.

QUESTIONS

7. As the Red Sox struggled through their decades-long World Series drought, how many consecutive postseason games did they lose between 1986 and 1995?

     A. 13

     B. 14

     C. 15

     D. 16

8. Roy Cullenbine, who played with MLB from 1938 to 1947, had a streak of how many consecutive games with a walk?

     A. 19

     B. 20

     C. 21

     D. 22

9. Carl Hubbell, pitcher for the New York Giants, won how many consecutive games over two seasons in 1936 and 1937?

     A. 19

     B. 22

     C. 24

     D. 27

ANSWERS

7.   A. 13

The Red Sox lost the World Series in 1986 to the New York Mets. In 1988 and 1990 they lost the American League Division Series—both times swept by the Oakland Athletics—and they lost the ALDS to the Cleveland Indians in 1995.

8.   D. 22

Cullenbine, who was known for his ability to draw walks, was playing with the Detroit Tigers when he walked in 22 games from July 2 to July 22, 1947.

9.   C. 24

Hubbell's winning streak, which lasted from July 18, 1936 until the following season on May 27, 1937, is still a record.

QUESTIONS

10. At the end of the 1988 season, how many consecutive scoreless innings did Los Angeles Dodger Orel Hershiser pitch?
  A. 48
  B. 51
  C. 56
  D. 59

11. How many consecutive shutouts did Don Drysdale pitch while playing for the Los Angeles Dodgers in 1968?
  A. Five
  B. Six
  C. Seven
  D. Eight

12. How long was the Boston Red Sox's World Series drought?
  A. 66 years
  B. 76 years
  C. 86 years
  D. 96 years

ANSWERS

10.   D. 59

Hershiser's streak lasted from August 30 until September 28, and he went on to lead the Dodgers to the 1988 World Series Championship. It should come as no surprise that he was named MVP!

11.   B. Six

The streak, which lasted from May 14 through June 4, resulted in 58 and two thirds consecutive scoreless innings pitched.

12.   C. 86 years

Two years after the Red Sox won the 1918 World Series, they sold Babe Ruth to the rival New York Yankees. As their World Series drought dragged on, some came to call it the "Curse of the Bambino" since it seemed to coincide with Ruth's departure. The Red Sox wouldn't win another series until 2004.

QUESTIONS

13. Which team has twice had a 12-game postseason winning streak?
        A. Atlanta Braves
        B. Boston Red Sox
        C. Los Angeles Dodgers
        D. New York Yankees

14. Which pitcher played an impressive 26 consecutive seasons with MLB?
        A. Nolan Ryan
        B. Randy Johnson
        C. Orel Hershiser
        D. Greg Maddux

15. Which first baseman faced 2,379 fielding chances without a single error?
        A. Lou Gehrig
        B. Casey Kotchman
        C. Jimmie Foxx
        D. Mark McGwire

ANSWERS

13.   D. New York Yankees

The Yankees won 12 straight postseason games in the 1927-28 seasons, and again in the 1998-99 seasons. They won the World Series all four years.

14.   A. Nolan Ryan

Ryan's long career was with the New York Mets, California Angels, Houston Astros, and Texas Rangers, and lasted from 1968 until 1993.

15.   B. Casey Kotchman

Kotchman's streak lasted from June 20, 2008 until August 21, 2010, while playing with the Angels, Braves, Red Sox, and Mariners.

QUESTIONS

16. Pitcher Terry Mulholland had an unusual streak: he played 12 consecutive seasons for different or multiple teams. For which team did he NOT pitch?

    A. New York Yankees

    B. Philadelphia Phillies

    C. Detroit Tigers

    D. Arizona Diamondbacks

17. How many consecutive seasons did Mariano Rivera appear in playoff games?

    A. 12

    B. 13

    C. 14

    D. 15

18. Which two pitchers won the Cy Young Award four years straight?

    A. Greg Maddux and Randy Johnson

    B. Randy Johnson and Nolan Ryan

    C. Nolan Ryan and Orel Hershiser

    D. Greg Maddux and Nolan Ryan

ANSWERS

16. C. Detroit Tigers

Mulholland also pitched for the Giants, Mariners, Cubs, Braves, Pirates, Dodgers, Indians, and Twins, between the years of 1993 and 2004.

17. B. 13

The New York Yankees closer appeared in the playoffs every year from his MLB debut in 1995 until 2007.

18. A. Greg Maddux and Randy Johnson

Maddux won from 1992 through 1995, while pitching for the Chicago Cubs and Atlanta Braves. Johnson won from 1999 to 2002, while playing with the Arizona Diamondbacks.

QUESTIONS

19. Sam Crawford, who played with MLB from 1899 to 1917, had a streak of three seasons hitting at least how many triples?

    A. 20

    B. 21

    C. 22

    D. 23

20. How many games did the Chicago Cubs win during their longest winning streak?

    A. 18

    B. 19

    C. 20

    D. 21

21. Which team made postseason appearances for 14 straight seasons?

    A. New York Yankees

    B. Atlanta Braves

    C. Boston Red Sox

    D. Cleveland Indians

ANSWERS

19. **A. 20**

Crawford accomplished the feat while playing with the Detroit Tigers from 1912 to 1914. The outfielder hit a total of 309 triples throughout his 19-season career.

20. **D. 21**

The Cubs won 21 games in a row during the 1935 season, from September 4 to September 28. They appeared in the World Series that year, but lost to the Detroit Tigers in six games.

21. **B. Atlanta Braves**

The Braves appeared in the postseason every year from 1991 to 2005, with the exception of the strike-cancelled 1994 season.

QUESTIONS

22. True or false:

Cal Ripken Jr. had another impressive streak in the middle of his consecutive-game streak.

23. True or false:

After the Oakland Athletics went on their amazing winning streak in 2002, they went on to play in the World Series.

24. True or false:

Although Cy Young holds the MLB record for most complete games pitched, he does not hold the record for consecutive complete games pitched.

25. True or false:

Ty Cobb, Babe Ruth, and Barry Bonds all achieved seven consecutive seasons with a slugging percentage of .600 or better.

26. True or false:

Speedy Rickey Henderson once boasted a streak of 12 consecutive games with a stolen base.

ANSWERS

22.   **True**

Ripken played 8,243 straight innings over 903 of those games. His streak-within-a-streak lasted from June 5, 1982 to September 14, 1987.

23.   **False**

The A's lost to the Minnesota Twins in the American League playoffs, and the Twins then lost to the Anaheim Angels. The Angels beat the San Francisco Giants to win the series that year.

24.   **True**

That pitching streak was accomplished by Jack Taylor, pitcher for the St. Louis Cardinals, between April 15 and October 6, 1904.

25.   **False**

Both Ruth and Bonds can boast the impressive achievement; however, although Ty Cobb is known for his career .367 batting average, he only broke a .600 slugging percentage one season.

26.   **False**

The feat was accomplished by shortstop Bert Campaneris of the Oakland Athletics between June 10 and June 21, 1969.

THE SCIENCE OF THE GAME

1. When a pitcher throws a 90-mph ball towards a batter, approximately how much time does the batter have to decide whether to swing or not?

 A. 0.2 seconds
 B. 0.5 seconds
 C. 1 second
 D. 1.2 seconds

2. How much time does it take for the sound from a batted ball to reach the ears of an outfielder?

 A. Instantaneously
 B. 0.1 seconds
 C. 0.3 seconds
 D. 0.5 seconds

3. How long does a typical swing of the bat last?

 A. 150 milliseconds
 B. 300 milliseconds
 C. 450 milliseconds
 D. 500 milliseconds

ANSWERS

1.   B. 0.5 seconds

In that split second, the batter must analyze the probable location of the ball and decide whether or not he'll be capable of hitting it.

2.   C. 0.3 seconds

An outfielder can often tell how well a ball was hit by listening to the sound it makes. So 0.3 seconds after a batter hits, the outfielder is reacting to the action.

3.   A. 150 milliseconds

In the first 50 of those 150 milliseconds, the batter can usually check his swing if he needs to; but after that, momentum will carry the bat around.

QUESTIONS

4. What is the fastest pitch ever thrown by pitching great Randy Johnson?
>A. 102 mph
>B. 103 mph
>C. 104 mph
>D. 105 mph

5. A batter must hit a ball within what margin of error to avoid hitting it foul?
>A. 5 milliseconds
>B. 14 milliseconds
>C. 18 milliseconds
>D. 21 milliseconds

6. How close must a ball be to the center of the baseball bat in order to result in a hit?
>A. ⅟₃₂ of an inch
>B. ⅟₁₆ of an inch
>C. ⅛ of an inch
>D. ¼ of an inch

ANSWERS

4.   A. 102 mph

40-year-old Johnson threw the pitch in 2004 while playing with the Arizona Diamondbacks.

5.   B. 14 milliseconds

Batters must hit a ball within a 14-millisecond window—too early or too late, and the ball will sail foul.

6.   C. ⅛ of an inch

Not only must the ball connect with the bat within an eighth of an inch of the center, but it must be hit at precisely the right millisecond!

QUESTIONS

7. The movement of a baseball when it is thrown or batted is a demonstration of what effect?

 A. Coriolis effect
 B. Dember effect
 C. Magnus effect
 D. Voigt effect

8. In 1974, which pitcher threw one of the fastest pitches ever recorded at more than 108 mph?

 A. Catfish Hunter
 B. Nolan Ryan
 C. Tom Seaver
 D. Jim Palmer

9. Approximately how much does a modern-day MLB bat weigh?

 A. 32 ounces
 B. 35 ounces
 C. 39 ounces
 D. 40 ounces

ANSWERS

7.   C. Magnus effect

In 1853, German physicist Gustav Magnus observed that rotating spherical objects reacted differently depending on which way they were spinning. This Magnus Effect is especially evident in pitching, where the spin on the ball makes the ball move in sometimes unpredictable ways.

8.   B. Nolan Ryan

The official speed of the pitch was a lightning-fast 108.1 mph – the fastest pitch ever recorded in an MLB game.

9.   A. 32 ounces

It is said that Babe Ruth used to use a bat that weighed around 43 ounces; but batters today prefer lighter bats because they can be swung faster.

QUESTIONS

10. A pitcher's arm acts as a what when he throws the ball?
    A. Gear
    B. Circuit
    C. Lever
    D. Pulley

11. The first baseball glove, which used felt and rubber padding to protect players' hands, was patented in what year?
    A. 1868
    B. 1885
    C. 1901
    D. 1910

12. How many miles per hour can a forward step add to a batter's swing?
    A. 10
    B. 12
    C. 14
    D. 16

ANSWERS

10.   C. Lever

A mechanical lever usually consists of a beam or rod attached at a fixed hinge, which pivots to create force. The pitcher's arm pivots at the shoulder, and creates force which is transferred into the thrown ball.

11.   B. 1885

The glove was invented by sporting goods store owner George H. Rawlings. Numerous other gloves have been invented since then, including one in 1896 that used compressed air to create a vacuum and trap the ball!

12.   A. 10

That forward step adds about 10 mph to a batter's swing. And by using his hips, a batter can add another 8 to 12 mph of forward speed.

QUESTIONS

13. From what part of the body does most of a pitcher's power originate?

      A. Legs

      B. Shoulders

      C. Arm

      D. Waist

14. What is the name for the mathematical and statistical analysis of baseball records?

      A. Factor analysis

      B. Sabermetrics

      C. Monte Carlo method

      D. Field analysis

15. Which of these factors can affect the distance a baseball can travel when hit?

      A. Humidity

      B. Temperature

      C. Altitude

      D. All of the above

ANSWERS

13.   D. Waist

Surprisingly, most of a pitcher's power comes from his core and not his arm. As he pitches, he bends forward at the waist, which provides power for his shoulder and arm. To demonstrate the difference, try throwing a ball while standing still, and then throw another while twisting and bending at the waist—the second ball should travel much farther!

14.   B. Sabermetrics

The name is derived from the acronym SABR, which stands for the Society of American Baseball Research. It was popularized in the 1970s by statistician Bill James, who also coined the term "sabermetrics."

15.   D. All of the above

Lower humidity, temperature, and altitude all result in more air resistance. Baseballs can be hit farther when the humidity, temperature, and altitude are higher.

QUESTIONS

16. True or false:
The raised stitching on a baseball creates drag that slows the ball down when it is pitched.

17. True or false:
It is best to attempt to hit a ball with a straight, level stroke of the bat.

18. True or false:
A ball hit from the "sweet spot" on a bat will cause more vibrations in the bat than a ball hit off another part of the bat.

19. True or false:
Nolan Ryan's 108.1-mph pitch was originally clocked at only 100.8 mph.

ANSWERS

16.   False

The stitching actually decreases the amount of the drag on the ball, because the raised surfaces decrease friction on the ball. A smooth ball wouldn't travel as far, because the friction against the smooth surface would cause more drag.

17.   False

According to Ted Williams and his hitting calculations, it is best to hit with a bit of an upstroke. This stroke, called "The Williams Stroke" matches the slight downward trajectory of the ball, increasing the area of contact.

18.   False

A well-hit ball causes fewer vibrations. This is one of the reasons a ball hit at the sweet spot will travel farther – there is no energy wasted in vibration, and all the energy goes into the flight of the ball.

19.   True

When the measurement was taken, the radar was set up to record speed only 10 feet from home plate. This meant that Ryan's pitch had 40 feet to slow down from its fastest velocity. When adjusted for today's measurements that are taken 50 feet from home plate, Ryan's pitch tops 108 mph.

SUPERSTITIONS

1. Hall of Famer Wade Boggs was known for doing what before games?

      A. Sitting in a hot tub

      B. Eating chicken

      C. Watching a movie

      D. Drinking coffee

2. What did first baseman Jason Giambi try in order to break out of slumps?

      A. Grew out his hair

      B. Switched out his bat

      C. Wore lucky underwear

      D. Stopped changing his socks

3. Relief pitcher Edward Mujica prefers what color Gatorade?

      A. Yellow

      B. Orange

      C. Blue

      D. Red

ANSWERS

1.   B. Eating chicken

Boggs' teammate on the Boston Red Sox, Jim Rice, used to call Boggs "chicken man."

2.   C. Wore lucky underwear

Giambi reportedly wore a "lucky" golden thong under his uniform to help him break out of slumps!

3.   D. Red

Mujica is very particular about the Gatorade he drinks. It has to be red, and during the fifth inning, he digs a small hole in front of the dugout and spits the Gatorade into it. Whatever works!

QUESTIONS

4. When Mark Teixeira played for the New York Yankees, he used to wear a sock with his number—25—on one foot, and whose sock on the other foot?

      A. CC Sabathia

      B. Robinson Cano

      C. Jorge Posada

      D. Derek Jeter

5. Which National League pitcher liked to name his bats after literary swords?

      A. Roy Halladay

      B. R.A. Dickey

      C. Jonathan Sanchez

      D. Ubaldo Jimenez

6. When Trevor Hoffman closed games for the San Diego Padres, what did the team's general manager, Kevin Towers, do?

      A. Lit candles

      B. Sat in the dugout

      C. Didn't watch

      D. Ate cookies

ANSWERS

4.   A. CC Sabathia

Sabathia—number 52—also got into the habit of wearing his own sock and one of Teixeira's. The routine began when Teixeria accidentally put on one of Sabathia's socks before a game and ended up with two home runs and six RBIs. The first baseman decided to continue wearing the 25/52 sock combo indefinitely.

5.   B. R.A. Dickey

Most players simply put their jersey numbers on their bats, but when Dickey played with the New York Mets, he gave his bats creative names. Two of them were called "Orcrist the Goblin Cleaver" and "Hrunting," named after swords used in the book The Hobbit *and the epic poem* Beowulf.

6.   C. Didn't watch

Hoffman was credited with 552 saves during his 16 years with the Padres, and Towers was convinced that the closer pitched better if he wasn't watching. Maybe it worked – Hoffman was the first closer to reach 500 and then 600 saves during his career.

QUESTIONS

7. What was the name of the curse that supposedly prevented the San Francisco Giants from winning the World Series until 2010?

    A. Curse of Coogan's Bluff

    B. Curse of the Bay City

    C. Curse of the Polo Grounds

    D. Curse of Nob Hill

8. Which pitcher is known to visit Popeye's Chicken before he starts a game?

    A. Zack Greinke

    B. Jon Lester

    C. Chris Sale

    D. Matt Garza

9. In 2008, what kind of good luck charm did the Los Angeles Dodgers have in their locker room?

    A. Snowglobe

    B. Garden gnome

    C. Coffeemaker

    D. Stuffed dog

ANSWERS

7.   A. Curse of Coogan's Bluff

The "curse" began when the Giants moved from New York to San Francisco in 1958. Angry fans in New York—who used to watch games at the Polo Grounds from a promontory overlooking the field called Coogan's Bluff—placed a hex on the new San Francisco team. They wouldn't win another World Series for 52 years.

8.   D. Matt Garza

Garza ate at the fried chicken restaurant before a game in 2008 when he pitched especially well. It's been a pre-game ritual ever since.

9.   B. Garden gnome

A Dodgers relief pitcher brought the garden gnome to the field when the pitching staff was slow to start. Eventually, the entire team rallied around the gnome, and by the end of the season, the Dodgers went from being in second-to-last place to first place in their division.

QUESTIONS

10. Pitcher Turk Wendell used to chew on what while he was pitching?

    A. Salt water taffy

    B. Black licorice

    C. Tobacco

    D. Sugarless gum

11. Many players have been known to wear necklaces made by the Japanese company Phiten that are laced with what metal?

    A. Titanium

    B. Copper

    C. Zinc

    D. Gold

12. Catcher Sherm Loller used to keep what in his locker for good luck?

    A. A picture of his wife

    B. A rabbit's foot

    C. Four-leaf clovers

    D. His first glove

ANSWERS

10.   B. Black licorice

Wendell, who pitched for the Cubs, Mets, Phillies, and Rockies, would chew exactly four pieces of the candy while he was on the mound. Between innings, he would spit it out, brush his teeth, and then grab four more pieces before he went out to pitch again. He also had a superstition about avoiding the foul line, and would jump high enough over it to avoid the dirt surrounding it, as well!

11.   A. Titanium

The metal in the necklaces is said to improve "quality of life" and give athletes an edge. Most experts agree that the edge is psychological, but that hasn't stopped players like Justin Verlander, C.J. Wilson, and Jon Lester from wearing the accessory.

12.   C. Four-leaf clovers

Perhaps they worked: Loller was a nine-time All Star and three-time Gold Glove Award winner. He also won two World Series championships: one in 1947 while playing with the New York Yankees, and one in 1966 while coaching for the Baltimore Orioles.

QUESTIONS

13. Outfielder Nyjer Morgan liked to wear blue argyle socks while playing for which team?
     A. Los Angeles Dodgers
     B. New York Mets
     C. Chicago Cubs
     D. Milwaukee Brewers

14. What flavor gum does utility player Elliot Johnson like to chew when his team takes the field?
     A. Mint
     B. Grape
     C. Bubblegum
     D. Cinnamon

15. When Joe DiMaggio ran from the outfield back to the dugout, what did he always make sure to touch?
     A. Second base
     B. First base
     C. The dugout ceiling
     D. The foul line

ANSWERS

13.   D. Milwaukee Brewers

Morgan's Twitter followers gave him the suggestion to wear blue argyle socks when the Brewers were in a slump. He wore the colorful footwear underneath his uniform socks.

14.   B. Grape

Johnson, who has played for the Rays, Royals, Braves, and Indians, likes to switch to watermelon-flavored gum when his team bats.

15.   A. Second base

The habit of stepping on second base on the way back to the dugout is a ritual that has been employed by many ballplayers over the years, but DiMaggio is especially famous for it.

QUESTIONS

16. Center fielder Steve Finley used to wear what for good luck?

       A. A broken watch

       B. A pouch of minerals

       C. A bandana

       D. Stickers on his helmet

17. When Roger Clemens pitched for the New York Yankees, what did he do before every game he started?

       A. Visited Monument Park

       B. Ate a pretzel

       C. Rode the elevated train

       D. Jogged once around the stadium

18. Richie Ashburn, who played in MLB from 1948 to 1962, would sometimes do what with his baseball bat?

       A. Wash it off in the shower

       B. Draw on it

       C. Sleep with it

       D. Use it as a doorstop

ANSWERS

16.   B. A pouch of minerals

Finley wore the pouch of minerals around his neck. He was so convinced of its positive influence that he persuaded his teammate, Darin Erstad, to wear one, too!

17.   A. Visited Monument Park

Clemens would go to Monument Park – an open-air museum at Yankee Stadium featuring plaques and monuments of past Yankees – and touch the bronze figure of Babe Ruth.

18.   C. Sleep with it

When Ashburn had a great game with a particular bat, he would take it with him between games to keep a close eye on it— even keeping it in his bed while he slept. He didn't trust that the clubhouse crew would give him the same bat at the next game, so he refused to let it out of his sight!

QUESTIONS

19. Andy Pettitte, who pitched for the New York Yankees and Houston Astros from 1995 to 2013, used to listen to the soundtrack of what movie before pitching?
>A. Rocky
>B. Jaws
>C. Die Hard
>D. The Terminator

20. Which center fielder was known to throw away his batting gloves every time he struck out?
>A. Carlos Beltran
>B. Kenny Lofton
>C. Lenny Dykstra
>D. Kirby Puckett

21. Relief pitcher Charlie Kerfeld always wore what when pitching?
>A. A pair of green socks
>B. A Jetsons t-shirt
>C. A yellow headband
>D. A Mickey Mouse watch

ANSWERS

19.   A. Rocky

*According to Luke Scott, Pettitte's teammate on the Astros,
the pitcher would listen to the entire soundtrack on game day,
because "it pumps him up."*

20.   C. Lenny Dykstra

*Dykstra, who played for the New York Mets and Philadelphia
Phillies, would get a new pair of batting gloves every time he
struck out.*

21.   B. A Jetsons t-shirt

*B. Kerfeld pitched for the Houston Astros from 1985 to 1990,
and wore the Jetsons shirt under his uniform for an obvious reason:
because the Jetsons' dog was named Astro!*

QUESTIONS

22. Legendary St. Louis Cardinal player Stan Musial used to eat what before each game?
> A. Turkey sandwich
> B. Eggs and pancakes
> C. Spaghetti
> D. Soup and salad

23. Which pitcher refused to wear more than one hat a year?
> A. Tom Glavine
> B. Kevin Millwood
> C. John Wetteland
> D. Pedro Martinez

24. The Curse of Rocky Colavito supposedly affects which team?
> A. San Diego Padres
> B. Chicago White Sox
> C. Houston Astros
> D. Cleveland Indians

ANSWERS

22.   B. Eggs and pancakes

Musial's breakfast wasn't very unusual, but he was particular about the way he ate it: he would start with an egg, then eat the pancakes, and then finish with one more egg.

23.   C. John Wetteland

Wetteland even refused to give up his single hat when he played in the World Series with the New York Yankees in 1996. Instead, he had the series logo sewn on to his well-worn hat!

24.   D. Cleveland Indians

The "curse" began when the Indians traded popular outfielder Rocky Colavito to the Detroit Tigers in 1960. It's said to prevent the team from even reaching the postseason, although the Indians have played in the World Series in 1995, 1997, and 2016. But—perhaps because of the curse?—they have lost all three series.

QUESTIONS

25. What did Atlanta Braves third baseman Chipper Jones like to do right before a game?
- A. Read a book
- B. Jump rope
- C. Call a friend
- D. Play computer solitaire

26. Which player refused to stand in the on-deck circle before batting?
- A. Ken Griffey Jr.
- B. Mark McGuire
- C. Adam Dunn
- D. Cecil Fielder

27. Outfielder Torii Hunter was known for his meticulously clean what?
- A. Shoes
- B. Helmet
- C. Fingernails
- D. Jersey

ANSWERS

25.   D. Play computer solitaire

Before night games, Jones would play solitaire until exactly 6:55, and then head to the dugout.

26.   C. Adam Dunn

Dunn, who played in MLB from 2001 to 2014, never liked the feel of the ground in the on-deck circle: "It's not the same consistency of dirt that there is in the batter's box," he says. Instead, he always chose to stand in the grass next to the on-deck circle.

27.   A. Shoes

Hunter would clean his shoes before every game, and then clean them again throughout the game as they got dirty.

QUESTIONS

28. True or false:

Superstitious Wade Boggs used to take batting practice at exactly 5:17.

29. True or false:

First baseman Adam LaRoche, who played in MLB from 2004 to 2015, was one of the most superstitious players in the majors during his career.

30. True or false:

Pitcher Max Scherzer has a superstition about talking about superstitions.

31. True or false:

Outfielder Jonny Gomes always put on his right socks and shoes before the left.

ANSWERS

28. **True**

Boggs also fielded exactly 150 balls during practice, and would run sprints at 7:17.

29. **False**

LaRoche made it a point to not participate in superstitious behavior throughout his career, not wanting to feel tied down to any ritual. "What if I wanted to go to my son's game, but I missed it because I have to go to the same sub shop for lunch every day at the same time?" he once said.

30. **True**

Scherzer, who has played for the Diamondbacks, Tigers, and Nationals, has his fair share of superstitious rituals: he eats a roast beef sandwich before each start, likes to flip the ball into his bare hand instead of his glove, and sometimes wears his shorts backwards. But according to those who know him, including teammates and his wife, Scherzer has many more superstitions but is too superstitious to talk about them!

31. **True**

Gomes, who played in MLB from 2003 to 2015, was adamant that when putting on anything in a pair—socks, shoes, even batting gloves—the right item had to be donned before the left.

LEGENDS

1. What was Yogi Berra's real name?

    A. Robert Anthony

    B. Harrison Lewis

    C. Lawrence Peter

    D. Gary James

2. What year did Jackie Robinson make his first appearance with MLB?

    A. 1946

    B. 1947

    C. 1948

    D. 1949

3. Outfielder and first baseman Stan Musial spent his entire 22-year career in MLB playing with which team?

    A. St. Louis Cardinals

    B. Brooklyn Dodgers

    C. Cleveland Indians

    D. Boston Red Sox

ANSWERS

1.   C. Lawrence Peter

One of Berra's childhood friends gave him the nickname "Yogi" because he liked to sit cross-legged—like a Hindu yogi.

2.   B. 1947

Due to segregation, Robinson had been forced to play with the Negro League Kansas City Monarchs for the first two years of his professional career. But on April 15, 1947, he broke the baseball color line and started at first base for the Brooklyn Dodgers.

3.   A. St. Louis Cardinals

Musial, nicknamed "Stan the Man," played with the Cardinals from 1941 to 1963, missing the 1945 season to serve in the Navy.

QUESTIONS

4. Baseball great Ty Cobb was born in which state?
- A. New York
- B. Florida
- C. Pennsylvania
- D. Georgia

5. In 2016, slugger Barry Bonds served as the hitting coach for which team?
- A. Miami Marlins
- B. Atlanta Braves
- C. San Diego Padres
- D. Chicago White Sox

6. Where was right fielder Roberto Clemente born?
- A. Venezuela
- B. Haiti
- C. Puerto Rico
- D. Dominican Republic

7. Who was known as "The Yankee Clipper"?
- A. Mickey Mantle
- B. Lou Gehrig
- C. Joe DiMaggio
- D. Babe Ruth

ANSWERS

4.   D. Georgia

Cobb, who was born Tyrus Raymond on December 18, 1886 in Narrows, Georgia, was nicknamed "The Georgia Peach."

5.   A. Miami Marlins

Although he was let go after the 2016 season, Bonds called the job "one of the most rewarding experiences of my baseball career."

6.   C. Puerto Rico

Clemente was born in Carolina, Puerto Rico.

7.   C. Joe DiMaggio

Stadium announcer Arch McDonald christened DiMaggio with the nickname, comparing his speed with the then-new "Clipper" airplanes flown by Pan Am.

QUESTIONS

8. What was Lou Gehrig's nickname?
A. The Legend
B. The Iron Horse
C. The Machine
D. The Captain

9. Alex Rodriguez played for three different teams in his 22-season career: the Seattle Mariners, New York Yankees, and who else?
A. Miami Marlins
B. Houston Astros
C. San Francisco Giants
D. Texas Rangers

10. How many Gold Glove awards did center fielder Willie Mays win?
A. 4
B. 7
C. 10
D. 12

ANSWERS

8. **B. The Iron Horse**

Gehrig earned the nickname during his 2,130-game playing streak, due to his tenacity and endurance. He played through a broken thumb, a broken toe, and back spasms, and an X-ray of his hands later revealed 17 separate fractures that had occurred and healed while he continued to play!

9. **D. Texas Rangers**

When Rodriguez signed with the Rangers for the 2001 season, his contract was the most lucrative sports contract ever signed. The shortstop was given a 10-year deal worth $252 million!

10. **D. 12**

This feat is especially notable since Mays' career began in 1951 and the Gold Glove award wasn't introduced until 1957. This means that over the last 17 years of his career—from 1957 until 1973— Mays won the award all but five times!

QUESTIONS

11. Where was New York Yankees shortstop Derek Jeter born?
- A. Ohio
- B. Michigan
- C. New York
- D. New Jersey

12. What was Cy Young's real name?
- A. Dennis Thomas
- B. Denton True
- C. Darnel Theodore
- D. Dalton Tobias

13. Babe Ruth began his career with which team?
- A. Boston Red Sox
- B. Brooklyn Dodgers
- C. New York Yankees
- D. Pittsburgh Pirates

ANSWERS

11.   D. New Jersey

Jeter was born on June 26, 1974 in Pequannock Township, New Jersey. His family later moved to Kalamazoo, Michigan, but Jeter spent summers in New Jersey with his grandparents, attending Yankees games and developing a love for baseball.

12.   B. Denton True

Denton True Young was born March 29, 1867, in Gilmore, Ohio. His nickname arose after a tryout for a minor league team, when he threw his pitches at a fence, and reporters observed that it "looked like a cyclone hit them." "Cyclone" was later shortened to "Cy," and Young used the nickname for the rest of his life.

13.   A. Boston Red Sox

Although best known as a slugger for the New York Yankees, Ruth began his baseball career as a pitcher for the Boston Red Sox.

QUESTIONS

14. Ty Cobb spent the majority of his career with the Detroit Tigers, but he also played with which team?
A. Pittsburgh Pirates
B. St. Louis Cardinals
C. Chicago White Sox
D. Philadelphia Athletics

15. For which team did Roberto Clemente play his entire career?
A. Pittsburgh Pirates
B. Philadelphia Phillies
C. Cleveland Indians
D. Atlanta Braves

16. In 1961, Mickey Mantle became the highest-paid active player in baseball. What was his yearly salary?
A. $50,000
B. $75,000
C. $100,000
D. $120,000

ANSWERS

14.   D. Philadelphia Athletics

Cobb retired after two seasons with the Athletics, where he hit his 4,000th hit off of pitcher Sam Gibson, a former Tigers teammate.

15.   A. Pittsburgh Pirates

Clemente spent 18 seasons playing for the Pirates, and his jersey number—21—was retired by the team in 1973.

16.   B. $75,000

Even adjusted for inflation, at around $600,000, this amount seems trivial compared to the baseball superstars of today. Mantle's highest salary was $100,000 a year, which he began making in 1963. He never asked for a pay raise the rest of his career.

QUESTIONS

17. Over the 22 seasons he played in MLB, how many seasons did Babe Ruth lead the American League in home runs?

     A. 6

     B. 9

     C. 12

     D. 14

18. Why didn't Sandy Koufax pitch game one of the 1965 World Series?

     A. It fell on Yom Kippur

     B. He broke his hand

     C. The game was rained out

     D. He was arrested the night before

19. Who broke Babe Ruth's single-season, 60-home-run record?

     A. Jackie Robinson

     B. Ted Williams

     C. Roger Maris

     D. Pete Rose

ANSWERS

17.   **C. 12**

Ruth logged 714 total home runs during his career, leading the league in 1918-1921, 1923, 1924, and 1926-1931.

18.   **A. It fell on Yom Kippur**

Koufax chose to observe the Jewish holiday of Yom Kippur, which fell on the same day as game one of the series between the Brooklyn Dodgers and the Minnesota Twins. He later pitched a complete game shutout in game five, and pitched another shutout in game seven on only two days' rest to clinch the series for the Dodgers.

19.   **C. Roger Maris**

Maris hit 61 home runs in 1961, breaking Ruth's 1927 record. Maris's record held until 1998, when Mark McGuire finished the season with 70 home runs, and Sammy Sosa ended up with 66.

QUESTIONS

20. Which player was a member of the first all African-American outfield in Major League history?

    A. Willie Mays

    B. Jackie Robinson

    C. Hank Aaron

    D. Ernie Banks

21. About how many MLB records did Ty Cobb set during the course of his career?

    A. 60

    B. 70

    C. 80

    D. 90

22. Which slugger became the youngest player ever to reach 500 home runs?

    A. Barry Bonds

    B. Pete Rose

    C. Alex Rodriguez

    D. Ken Griffey Jr.

ANSWERS

20. A. Willie Mays

Mays, along with Hank Thompson and Monte Irvin, covered the outfield for the New York Giants in the 1951 World Series.

21. D. 90

Cobb is credited with 90 different records. Some of them still stand, including his highest career batting average of .367 and his record-setting 54 stolen home bases.

22. C. Alex Rodriguez

Rodriguez hit his 500th home run on August 4, 2007, when he was just 32 years, eight days old.

QUESTIONS

23. In which state was center fielder Mickey Mantle born?
   A. New Jersey
   B. Oklahoma
   C. Ohio
   D. Nevada

24. Which team was Pete Rose playing for when he hit his 4000th career hit?
   A. Cincinnati Reds
   B. Montreal Expos
   C. Chicago Cubs
   D. Philadelphia Phillies

25. Which player was known by the nickname "The Flying Dutchman"?
   A. Rogers Hornsby
   B. Joe DiMaggio
   C. Ty Cobb
   D. Honus Wagner

ANSWERS

23.   B. Oklahoma

Mantle was born on October 20, 1931, in Spavinaw, Oklahoma. His father named him in honor of Hall of Fame catcher Mickey Cochrane.

24.   B. Montreal Expos

Although Rose is best known for his time with the Cincinnati Reds, he also played with the Philadelphia Phillies from 1979 to 1983, and spent a single season with the Expos in 1984.

25.   D. Honus Wagner

Wagner played in MLB from 1897 to 1917, for the Louisville Colonels and the Pittsburgh Pirates. His nickname was partly thanks to his speed, and also a nod to the opera The Flying Dutchman by another famous Wagner: German composer Richard Wagner.

QUESTIONS

26. What was Lou Gehrig's jersey number?

      A. 2

      B. 4

      C. 6

      D. 8

27. In addition to the Baseball Hall of Fame, Ted Williams was inducted into which other hall of fame?

      A. National Aviation Hall of Fame

      B. International Bowling Hall of Fame

      C. International Game Fish Association Hall of Fame

      D. California Hall of Fame

28. How old was Connie Mack when he retired from managing the Philadelphia Athletics?

      A. 59

      B. 65

      C. 73

      D. 87

ANSWERS

26. **B. 4**

Gehrig's number was retired by the New York Yankees in 1939, when he was forced to retire from the game due to amyotrophic lateral sclerosis (ALS).

27. **C. International Game Fish Association Hall of Fame**

Williams was an avid sport fisherman, and he spent much of his time after retiring from baseball fishing the Miramichi River in New Brunswick, Canada. He was inducted into the IGFA Hall of Fame in 2000.

28. **D. 87**

Mack was the longest-serving manager in MLB history, spending an amazing 50 seasons with the Athletics.

QUESTIONS

29. Who was known by the nickname "The Grey Eagle"?
    A. Lou Gehrig
    B. Tris Speaker
    C. Pete Rose
    D. Sandy Koufax

30. Which team passed over Derek Jeter in the 1992 MLB draft, against the advice of former Detroit Tigers pitcher Hal Newhouser?
    A. Cleveland Indians
    B. Seattle Mariners
    C. Chicago White Sox
    D. Houston Astros

31. Which two players are the only ones to have won the Triple Crown twice in their careers?
    A. Rogers Hornsby and Ted Williams
    B. Mickey Mantle and Ted Williams
    C. Babe Ruth and Hank Aaron
    D. Hank Aaron and Rogers Hornsby

ANSWERS

29.   B. Tris Speaker

Speaker, who still holds a career record for doubles with 792, got his nickname due to his prematurely grey hair.

30.   D. Houston Astros

Newhouser worked as a scout for the Astros, and was convinced that Jeter would be an asset to the team. But the Astros, worried that Jeter would ask for too much money, instead went with Phil Nevin. Newhouser disagreed so strongly with their decision that he quit his job.

31.   A. Rogers Hornsby and Ted Williams

Hornsby won in 1922 and 1925; Williams won in 1942 and 1947.

QUESTIONS

32. True or false:
Babe Ruth was not a very good pitcher, even though that is how he began his career.

33. True or false:
After his baseball career, Jackie Robinson had the distinction of becoming the first black vice president of a major American corporation.

34. True or false:
As of the end of the 2016 season, Barry Bonds was the sole member of the "500-500" club.

35. True or false:
Ty Cobb left the Detroit Tigers near the end of his career because he felt he wasn't paid enough.

ANSWERS

32. False

Ruth was actually quite a stellar pitcher for the Red Sox, with a 94-46 win-loss record and a very respectable 2.28 ERA. He was the American League ERA leader in 1916, and helped the Red Sox win World Series victories in 1915, 1916, and 1918; the latter would be the last win for the Red Sox until 2004, thanks to the Curse of the Bambino!

33. True

In the 1950s, Robinson became vice president and director of personnel at coffee company Chock Full o'Nuts.

34. True

The distinction means that he is the only player so far to have hit at least 500 home runs and steal at least 500 bases.

35. False

Cobb was forced to quietly retire from the Tigers in 1926 after a former pitcher named Dutch Leonard accused him of gambling and fixing games. The allegations turned out to be false, and Cobb was cleared of any wrongdoing. He was allowed to return to MLB as a free agent, and signed with the Philadelphia Athletics.

EAT, DRINK, & PLAY BALL!

....

1. In what year was salty and sweet Cracker Jack introduced to consumers?

      A. 1896

      B. 1901

      C. 1908

      D. 1915

2. A popular hot dog myth credits the name "hot dog" to a cartoonist who attended a ballgame at which park?

      A. Washington Park

      B. Ebbets Field

      C. Fenway Park

      D. Polo Grounds

ANSWERS

1.   A. 1896

Brothers Frederick and Louis Rueckheim created the treat, which consisted of popcorn and peanuts coated in molasses. One of their first product testers proclaimed that the snack was "crackerjack," which, at the time, was slang for "excellent."

2.   D. Polo Grounds

As the story goes, the cartoonist was attending a New York Giants game and saw a vendor selling "hot dachshund sausages." The cartoonist drew a picture of a dachshund in a bun, but couldn't spell "dachshund"—so he simply wrote "hot dog." Although it's a great story, there has never been any proof that it actually happened!

QUESTIONS

3. Which former major leaguer opened a barbecue stand at the Baltimore Orioles' Camden Yards?

      A. Jim Palmer

      B. Boog Powell

      C. Cal Ripken Jr.

      D. Frank Robinson

4. Which team offers something called a "burgerizza"?

      A. Atlanta Braves

      B. New York Mets

      C. Los Angeles Dodgers

      D. Chicago White Sox

5. Fans can eat a chicken and waffle on a stick when they're watching which team play?

      A. San Diego Padres

      B. Miami Marlins

      C. Toronto Blue Jays

      D. Cleveland Indians

ANSWERS

3.   B. Boog Powell

John Wesley "Boog" Powell was a first baseman for the Orioles from 1961 to 1974, where he was a four-time All Star and two-time World Series champion.

4.   A. Atlanta Braves

As the name suggests, the "burgerizza" is a hamburger patty, topped with cheese and bacon, sandwiched between two pizzas!

5.   C. Toronto Blue Jays

The deep-fried chicken and waffle stick comes with Sriracha maple syrup and broccoli and cabbage slaw.

QUESTIONS

6. The Texas Rangers added a colossal sandwich to their concession lineup with pulled pork, bacon, prosciutto, sausage, ham, and pork rinds, called the what?

    A. Mr. Piggy

    B. Heart Attack

    C. Wicked Pig

    D. Food Coma

7. Which team features Gilroy Garlic Fries?

    A. San Diego Padres

    B. San Francisco Giants

    C. Los Angeles Dodgers

    D. Los Angeles Angels of Anaheim

8. In 2016, the New York Yankees introduced a sandwich that includes a burger, fried chicken cutlet, and hash browns, called what?

    A. Barnyard Wedding

    B. Kitchen Sink

    C. Arranged Marriage

    D. Down on the Farm

ANSWERS

6.   **C. Wicked Pig**

All of that pork is piled between Hawaiian rolls and topped with coleslaw. The gigantic sandwich costs $27!

7.   **B. San Francisco Giants**

Fans of the Giants are also huge fans of the fries, which take their name from the town of Gilroy, California—"the garlic capital of the world." They're covered in garlic, olive oil, and parsley, and come with a complimentary breath mint!

8.   **A. Barnyard Wedding**

The Barnyard Wedding sandwich is topped off with barbecue sauce and cheddar cheese.

QUESTIONS

9. Whose fans can chow down on Wazee Market sandwiches?

       A. Colorado Rockies

       B. Houston Astros

       C. Cleveland Indians

       D. Chicago Cubs

10. The Los Angeles Dodgers offer a snack called elote, which is what?

       A. Spicy chickpeas

       B. Sweetened pastries

       C. Grilled corn

       D. Fried potatoes

11. In 2016, the Pittsburgh Pirates began offering a hot dog covered in which two other snack foods?

       A. Potato chips and chili

       B. Mac & cheese and Cracker Jack

       C. Bacon and chocolate

       D. Pickles and cheese puffs

ANSWERS

9.   A. Colorado Rockies

The sandwiches are named after a Denver produce market that was popular from the 1940s to the early 1970s. Fans can also order pizza and gelato at the stadium shop.

10.   C. Grilled corn

The Mexican-style grilled corn is lightly coated with mayonnaise and sprinkled with chile powder and cheese.

11.   B. Mac & cheese and Cracker Jack

While the mac and cheese might make some sense as a hot dog topper, many fans were confused by the addition of Cracker Jack. Pittsburgh Post-Gazette blogger Alex Iniguez called the offering "an abomination" and "utterly ridiculous"!

QUESTIONS

12. In 2015, the Texas Rangers introduced a hot dog topped with what unusual ingredient?
      A. Cotton candy
      B. Rice Krispies
      C. Granola
      D. Licorice

13. The Cleveland Indians also have a strange culinary combination for fans to try: French fries topped with what?
      A. Soft serve
      B. Sliced fruit
      C. Almond butter
      D. Caramel

14. Fans of which team used to enjoy a famous sandwich called the Schmitter?
      A. Chicago Cubs
      B. Atlanta Braves
      C. Philadelphia Phillies
      D. Colorado Rockies

ANSWERS

12.   A. Cotton candy

The strange combination came about when a concessions manager saw first baseman Prince Fielder eating cotton candy, and decided to try it on top of a hot dog. Amazingly, fans have called the combo "surprisingly delicious."

13.   D. Caramel

Cleveland Caramel Fries were created when a concessions manager asked his team to top fries with whatever they could find in the kitchen. They ended up drizzling the fried potatoes with caramel, chocolate, and whipped cream.

14.   C. Philadelphia Phillies

The sandwich featured roast beef, salami, cheese, sliced tomato and onion, and a special sauce, all on a Kaiser roll. As of 2016, the iconic sandwich was removed from the concession offerings at the stadium when the sandwich shop lost its location in the concourse. But management is hopeful that it will eventually return.

QUESTIONS

15. Where can you find tempura-battered burgers and hot dogs to nosh on during the game?
A. Kansas City
B. Miami
C. Seattle
D. Houston

16. Fans can chow down on a 108 Burger while watching which team play?
A. Arizona Diamondbacks
B. Los Angeles Dodgers
C. New York Mets
D. Pittsburgh Pirates

17. Which team features Mexican fare from local restaurant Chronic Tacos?
A. Houston Astros
B. Los Angeles Angels of Anaheim
C. Tampa Bay Rays
D. San Diego Padres

ANSWERS

15. **A. Kansas City**

The burger and hot dog both come with sweet coleslaw and chipotle ketchup on locally made buns.

16. **C. New York Mets**

The 108 Burger takes a regular burger and gives it some New York flair, with hot pastrami, deli mustard, Havarti cheese, and a pretzel roll.

17. **B. Los Angeles Angels of Anaheim**

The popular California eatery serves Angels fans tacos and tostada bowls to enjoy with the game.

QUESTIONS

18. The Chicago White Sox sell a sundae in a full-size batting helmet with how many scoops of ice cream?
- A. 8
- B. 10
- C. 12
- D. 14

19. Which culinary offering is quickly gaining popularity at Fenway Park?
- A. Barbecue nachos
- B. Spicy hot chocolate
- C. Lobster rolls
- D. Veggie burgers

ANSWERS

18.   **C. 12**

The huge sundae has 12 scoops of vanilla, chocolate, and strawberry ice cream, plus strawberry and chocolate sauce, bananas, whipped cream, and cherries. The whole thing weighs three pounds!

19.   **C. Lobster rolls**

Although the Fenway Frank is still king, the lobster roll is a close second. The fresh Maine lobster is cooked prior to each game, and tossed with butter, mayo, tarragon, celery, chives, and sea salt, and served on a hot dog bun.

QUESTIONS

20. True or false:
Cracker Jack mascot Sailor Jack once threw out the ceremonial first pitch at an MLB game.

21. True or false:
Every individual MLB stadium controls the concessions offered to fans.

22. True or false:
A single man was able to eat an entire Chicago White Sox batting helmet sundae in under three minutes.

23. True or false:
One of the most famous offerings at the Cleveland Indians ballpark is a condiment.

ANSWERS

20. True

The Chicago Cubs celebrated the 100th anniversary of Cracker Jack at Wrigley Field on June 16, 1993, where the mascot threw out the first pitch.

21. False

Six companies—Aramark, Delaware North, Levy, Centerplate, Legends, and Ovations Food Services—control the food offerings at every one of the 30 MLB stadiums. These same companies also have concessions contracts with other sporting arenas, minor league stadiums, and airports.

22. True

Patrick Bertoletti is a competitive eater from Chicago, who, during the course of his unusual career, has managed to eat 55 hot dogs in 10 minutes, 94 hamburgers in eight minutes, and 21 pounds of grits in 10 minutes (among many other culinary obliterations!). He finished the three-pound White Sox sundae—which is plenty to feed four or five people—in two minutes, 53 seconds!

23. True

The Cleveland Indians have served Bertman Original Ball Park Mustard for more than 90 years, which fans claim is the best mustard to slather on a hot dog on game day!

MOVIES

BULL DURHAM

1. Kevin Costner—who has quite a few baseball movies in his résumé—plays the part of Crash Davis in 1988's *Bull Durham*. But who was originally tapped for the part?

    A. Bruce Willis

    B. Kurt Russell

    C. Dennis Quaid

    D. Gary Sinise

2. The film was nominated for how many Oscars?

    A. One

    B. Two

    C. Three

    D. None

3. Which actress stars as English professor and baseball fan Annie Savoy?

    A. Debra Winger

    B. Rene Russo

    C. Ellen Barkin

    D. Susan Sarandon

ANSWERS

1.   **B. Kurt Russell**

Russell helped writer Ron Shelton develop the script, and was reportedly quite impressed with the final choice of Costner for the part of Crash.

2.   **A. One**

Ron Shelton was nominated in 1989 for best original screenplay for Bull Durham.

3.   **D. Susan Sarandon**

Sarandon starred with her real-life partner, Tim Robbins, who played the part of Ebby Calvin "Nuke" LaLoosh. Sarandon and Robbins have stated that Bull Durham *is their favorite film that they've made together.*

QUESTIONS

4. What was Crash Davis's jersey number?

    A. 2

    B. 5

    C. 8

    D. 11

5. During the "conversation on the mound" scene, what does coach Larry Hockett say makes a good wedding gift?

    A. Candlesticks

    B. Picture frames

    C. A toaster

    D. Money

6. The Durham Bulls are a real minor league team in North Carolina. At the time of filming, which major league team were they affiliated with?

    A. Pittsburgh Pirates

    B. Baltimore Orioles

    C. Atlanta Braves

    D. Miami Marlins

ANSWERS

4.   **C. 8**

Writer Ron Shelton was a former minor league baseball player himself, who drew on his past experience when writing the story. The last number he wore when he played was 8, so the costume designer for the film gave Crash Davis the same number.

5.   **A. Candlesticks**

According to actor Robert Wuhl, who played the part of Larry, he improvised the "candlesticks" line, saying he based it on a conversation he had with his wife.

6.   **C. Atlanta Braves**

When the film was released in 1988, the Durham Bulls were a single-A affiliate of the Atlanta Braves. But as of 2013, the Bulls are now a triple-A affiliate of the Tampa Bay Rays.

FIELD OF DREAMS

1. The 1989 film *Field of Dreams* was based on a book by which author?
     A. Chad Harbach
     B. Philip Roth
     C. W.P. Kinsella
     D. Bernard Malamud

2. In which state does the film take place?
     A. Iowa
     B. Nebraska
     C. Illinois
     D. Kansas

3. In the film, Kevin Costner's character, Ray Kinsella, kidnaps reclusive writer Terrance Mann. But who did the character kidnap in the original story?
     A. Harper Lee
     B. J.D. Salinger
     C. Hunter S. Thompson
     D. Thomas Pynchon

ANSWERS

1.   C. W.P. Kinsella

Kinsella's book was titled Shoeless Joe, *but test audiences for the movie didn't like it as a film title, thinking that anyone unfamiliar with baseball might think it was a movie about a hobo! So the title was changed to* Field of Dreams, *which Kinsella approved. In fact, he had considered calling his book* Dream Field.

2.   A. Iowa

The baseball diamond used for filming was built on an actual farm in Dubuque County, Iowa. After filming, the family who owned the farm kept the baseball diamond and added a small stand for souvenirs. As of today, more than one million fans have visited the site, which is open daily from April through October.

3.   B. J.D. Salinger

The famously secluded J.D. Salinger was not happy when he read about himself in Kinsella's Shoeless Joe, *and lawyers threatened to sue if he used Salinger in the film version of the story. So instead, Kinsella created fictional "reclusive writer" Terrance Mann, played by James Earl Jones.*

A LEAGUE OF THEIR OWN

1. Who directed the 1992 film *A League of Their Own?*
  A. Rob Reiner
  B. Penny Marshall
  C. Nora Ephron
  D. Garry Marshall

2. In what year does the film take place?
  A. 1941
  B. 1942
  C. 1943
  D. 1944

3. Which actor plays washed-up ballplayer Jimmy Dugan?
  A. Jim Belushi
  B. Bill Pullman
  C. Ray Liotta
  D. Tom Hanks

ANSWERS

1.   B. Penny Marshall

Marshall, who also directed Big, Awakenings, *and* The Preacher's Wife, *is a lifelong baseball fan who was inspired to make the film after watching a documentary about the All-American Girls Professional Baseball League.*

2.   C. 1943

This was the year the All-American Girls Professional Baseball League made its debut, as a way to maintain the popularity of baseball while many men were overseas. The AAGPBL lasted until 1954.

3.   D. Tom Hanks

Hanks had to gain 30 pounds to play the out-of-shape Dugan, which he accomplished by frequenting a nearby Dairy Queen. Eight years later, Hanks famously lost 50 pounds to play a marooned plane crash survivor in Cast Away.

QUESTIONS

4. Which actress plays catcher Dottie Hinson?
    A. Kelly McGillis
    B. Geena Davis
    C. Demi Moore
    D. Sean Young

5. Who plays baseball scout Ernie Capadino?
    A. Christopher Walken
    B. Jim Belushi
    C. Joe Pesci
    D. Jon Lovitz

6. Dottie's sister, Kit—played by actress Lori Petty—likes to swing at what kind of pitches?
    A. Fastballs
    B. High balls
    C. Curveballs
    D. Low balls

7. True or false:
    The bumps, bruises, and scrapes seen in the film were all real injuries sustained by the actresses.

ANSWERS

4.   B. Geena Davis

Davis's character was based on real-life AAGPBL pitcher Dottie Collins. Throughout her six-year career, Collins had a 177-76 win-loss record, threw 1,205 strikeouts, and had an ERA of 1.83.

5.   D. Jon Lovitz

The part of the cigar-smoking, sarcastic baseball scout was written specifically with Lovitz in mind.

6.   B. High balls

Kit says she "likes the high ones" but usually strikes out when she tries to hit them. At the end of the film, she swings at another high pitch, but manages to hit it, ultimately winning the game for her team.

7. True

All of the actresses in the movie played actual games of baseball and learned to hit, field, and slide into bases. The bruises and scrapes seen on-screen were all real!

MAJOR LEAGUE

1. Which MLB team is represented in the 1989 film *Major League?*
      A. Cincinnati Reds
      B. Philadelphia Phillies
      C. Chicago Cubs
      D. Cleveland Indians

2. Who plays Jake Taylor, the catcher with bad knees?
      A. Tom Berenger
      B. Corbin Bernsen
      C. Dennis Haysbert
      D. Jeff Bridges

3. Which real-life MLB ballplayer has a memorable role in Major League?
      A. Pete Rose
      B. Lou Piniella
      C. Bob Uecker
      D. Tom Seaver

ANSWERS

1.   D. Cleveland Indians

In the movie, the owner of the Indians, Rachel Phelps (played by Margaret Whitton), hires terrible players so the team will lose and she can move them to Miami. Of course, her plot ends up backfiring in hilarious ways!

2.   A. Tom Berenger

Berenger has appeared in scores of films and television shows, including The Big Chill, Platoon, *and* Inception, *as well as reprising his role of Jake Taylor in* Major League II.

3.   C. Bob Uecker

Uecker, who was an MLB catcher from 1962 to 1967, plays Indians announcer Harry Doyle. He was encouraged to ad lib some of his lines, including the famous "just a bit outside" quip.

EIGHT MEN OUT

1. In what year does the 1988 drama *Eight Men Out* take place?

    A. 1901
    B. 1909
    C. 1919
    D. 1925

2. Who directed the film?

    A. John Sayles
    B. Phil Alden Robinson
    C. Sam Raimi
    D. David Ward

3. Actor John Cusack portrays which White Sox player?

    A. Arnold Gandil
    B. Joseph Sullivan
    C. Eddie Cicotte
    D. George Weaver

ANSWERS

1.   C. 1919

The film tells the story of the 1919 Black Sox scandal, when eight Chicago White Sox players deliberately threw the World Series to benefit gamblers.

2.   A. John Sayles

Sayles often appears in the films he directs, with parts in Lianna, City of Hope, Sunshine State, *and* Eight Men Out, *where he plays newspaper writer Ring Lardner.*

3.   D. George Weaver

Weaver, a shortstop and third baseman, batted .324 with 11 hits and no errors in the 1919 World Series, an unusual record for someone who supposedly helped throw the series. For his entire life, he swore he had nothing to do with the scandal, and tried unsuccessfully to be reinstated to baseball.

QUESTIONS

4. Which player is brought to life by actor Charlie Sheen?
    A. Eddie Cicotte
    B. Happy Felsch
    C. Charles Risberg
    D. Lefty Williams

5. Actor D.B. Sweeney plays which member of the White Sox team?
    A. Shoeless Joe Jackson
    B. Lefty Williams
    C. Arnold Gandil
    D. Charles Risberg

ANSWERS

4.   B. Happy Felsch

Oscar "Happy" Felsch was one of the best hitters in the American League throughout the five years he played for the White Sox. His poor performance and many errors during the 1919 World Series left little doubt that he was involved in the Black Sox scandal.

5.   A. Shoeless Joe Jackson

Jackson played in MLB for 12 years, playing with the Philadelphia Athletics and the Cleveland Indians before joining the White Sox. His exemplary performance during the 1919 World Series— where he hit .375, had 12 hits, and no errors—led many to believe that he was innocent of involvement in the scandal.

THE NATURAL

1. Who directed the 1984 drama *The Natural*, based on the novel by Bernard Malamud?
   A. Bennett Miller
   B. Barry Levinson
   C. Phil Alden Robinson
   D. Sam Raimi

2. In what year does most of the story take place?
   A. 1935
   B. 1937
   C. 1939
   D. 1941

3. The film was nominated for how many Academy Awards?
   A. Three
   B. Four
   C. Five
   D. Six

ANSWERS

1.   B. Barry Levinson

Levinson is also known for directing Diner, Rain Man, Toys, *and* Good Morning, Vietnam.

2.   C. 1939

1939 was considered the 100th anniversary of professional organized baseball. It was also the year the National Baseball Hall of Fame was established in Cooperstown, New York.

3.   B. Four

The Natural *was nominated for Best Music, Best Art Direction, Best Cinematography, and Best Actress in a Supporting Role (for Glenn Close's portrayal of Iris Gaines).*

QUESTIONS

4. Actor Robert Redford plays a mysterious, middle-aged rookie named what?

    A. Ron Hayes

    B. Rob Harris

    C. Roy Hobbs

    D. Rip Hill

5. The cast of the film includes three Oscar winners: Robert Redford, Robert Duvall, and who else?

    A. Kim Basinger

    B. Mary Steenburgen

    C. Geena Davis

    D. Frances McDormand

6. True or false:

    The storyline where Hobbs is shot by an obsessed fan (played by Barbara Hershey) was based on a true event.

ANSWERS

4.   C. Roy Hobbs

Reportedly, Redford looked to Ted Williams when he modeled Roy Hobbs' swing of the bat. Hobbs also wears number 9—the same number Williams wore—and both hit home runs in their last career at-bats.

5.   A. Kim Basinger

Redford won a Best Director Oscar in 1981 for Ordinary People; *Duvall won a Best Actor Oscar in 1984 for* Tender Mercies; *and Basinger won a Best Actress Oscar in 1998 for* L.A. Confidential.

6.   True

On June 14, 1949, star Philadelphia Phillies first baseman Eddie Waitkus was shot by an obsessed fan named Ruth Ann Steinhagen in a Chicago hotel. Waitkus survived and fought his way back into playing shape, leading the Phillies in scoring with 102 runs in his return season in 1950. Steinhagen was committed to a psychiatric hospital after the shooting, and was released in 1952. Waitkus declined pressing charges, saying he wanted to forget about the incident, and Steinhagen quietly lived the rest of her life with family in Chicago.

THE PRIDE OF THE YANKEES

1. What year was the Lou Gehrig biopic *The Pride of the Yankees* released?
>   A. 1942
>   B. 1943
>   C. 1944
>   D. 1945

2. Which actor plays the Yankee legend?
>   A. Clark Gable
>   B. Cary Grant
>   C. Gary Cooper
>   D. James Stewart

3. Which actress plays Gehrig's wife, Eleanor?
>   A. Virginia Gilmore
>   B. Joan Leslie
>   C. Jean Arthur
>   D. Teresa Wright

ANSWERS

1.   A. 1942

The film premiered just 13 months after Gehrig succumbed to ALS on June 2, 1941.

2.   C. Gary Cooper

Cooper, who appeared in classics like High Noon, Mr. Deeds Goes to Town, *and* Sergeant York, *wasn't a fan of baseball when he made the film. In fact, he'd never even seen a live game, and had to train extensively to be believable in the role.*

3.   D. Teresa Wright

Wright received her third consecutive Academy Award nomination for The Pride of the Yankees, *which was only the third film of her career. She is the only actress to ever receive nominations for her first three films.*

4 2

1. In 2013's drama *42*, which actor plays baseball great Jackie Robinson?

     A. Brandon T. Jackson

     B. Chadwick Boseman

     C. Mehcad Brooks

     D. Edi Gathegi

2. The film was written and directed by Brian Helgeland, who also wrote which Oscar-winning screenplay?

     A. *Sling Blade*

     B. *The Cider House Rules*

     C. *A Beautiful Mind*

     D. *L.A. Confidential*

3. Which actor plays MLB executive Branch Rickey?

     A. Robert Duvall

     B. Ben Kingsley

     C. Harrison Ford

     D. Christopher Walken

ANSWERS

1.   **B. Chadwick Boseman**

Boseman has appeared in television shows like Lincoln Heights *and* Persons Unknown, *and in the films* Draft Day, Gods of Egypt, *and* Captain America: Civil War.

2.   **D. L.A. Confidential**

Helgeland, along with writer Curtis Hanson, won the Oscar for Best Adapted Screenplay in 1998. He is also known for his work on A Knight's Tale, Mystic River, Robin Hood, *and* Legend.

3.   **C. Harrison Ford**

Branch Rickey—who also drafted the first Hispanic MLB star, Roberto Clemente—was the first real-life person Ford ever portrayed in film.

MONEYBALL

1. The 2011 film *Moneyball* depicts the struggles of which team?
     A. San Diego Padres
     B. Oakland Athletics
     C. Seattle Mariners
     D. Houston Astros

2. Who directed the film?
     A. Ron Shelton
     B. David Ward
     C. Stan Dragoti
     D. Bennett Miller

3. In which year does the story take place?
     A. 1995
     B. 1999
     C. 2002
     D. 2006

ANSWERS

1.   B. Oakland Athletics

The film is based on a book of the same name by author Michael Lewis, and recounts the A's struggle to build a better team despite having one of the lowest budgets in baseball.

2.   D. Bennett Miller

Miller has been nominated for two Oscars for Best Director: one for 2005's Capote, *and one for 2014's* Foxcatcher.

3.   C. 2002

Moneyball *recounts the A's record-breaking 2002 season, when they won an amazing 20 games in a row and made it to the postseason.*

QUESTIONS

4. Which actor plays the Oakland A's general manager, Billy Beane?

      A. Robert Downey Jr.

      B. Brad Pitt

      C. Scott Bakula

      D. Denzel Washington

5. Who plays assistant general manager Peter Brand?

      A. Jonah Hill

      B. Chris Hemsworth

      C. Charlie Cox

      D. Seth Rogen

6. Which popular actor appears as first baseman Scott Hatteberg?

      A. Ryan Gosling

      B. Chris Pine

      C. Chris Pratt

      D. Channing Tatum

ANSWERS

4.   B. Brad Pitt

In 2011, Pitt stared in Moneyball *and the drama* The Tree of Life, *both of which were nominated for Best Picture Oscars. Pitt was also nominated for Best Actor for his role as Billy Beane.*

5.   A. Jonah Hill

Hill, who is best known for his comedic roles in films like Superbad, Get Him to the Greek, *and* 21 Jump Street, *was nominated for a Best Supporting Actor Oscar for his role in* Moneyball.

6.   C. Chris Pratt

At Pratt's first audition for the role, he was told that he weighed too much to be believable as a professional ballplayer. So he began losing weight, hoping to get in shape before the part was cast. His dedication paid off: he lost weight, and got the part!

THE ROOKIE

1. The 2002 film *The Rookie* tells the true story of which MLB relief pitcher?

        A. Keith Foulke

        B. Jim Morris

        C. Robb Nen

        D. Derek Lowe

2. Who plays the part of high school baseball coach and eventual MLB pitcher Jim Morris?

        A. Dennis Quaid

        B. Kevin Costner

        C. Corbin Bernsen

        D. Bill Paxton

3. In which state does Jim Morris live and coach baseball?

        A. Iowa

        B. Florida

        C. New Jersey

        D. Texas

ANSWERS

1.   **B. Jim Morris**

Morris spent less than a year pitching for the Tampa Bay Devil Rays, from September 1999 to May 2000.

2.   **A. Dennis Quaid**

Quaid did much of the pitching in the film himself, with the exception of scenes that required high-speed fastballs. Those pitches were thrown by minor league pitcher Jeff Dowdy.

3.   **D. Texas**

Morris teaches high school science in Big Lake, Texas. While coaching the school's baseball team, he makes a promise to try out for professional baseball if they win a championship. The team wins, and Morris makes good on his promise.